DK GIRL WORLD

Quiz Zone

DK GIRL WORLD

Quiz Zone

50 Quizzes to **Unravel** Your Future, **Reveal** Your Style and **Discover** the Inner You!

by **Michelle Hainer**

Illustrations by Georgia Rucker

DK

LONDON, NEW YORK, MUNICH, MELBOURNE AND DELHI

Senior Editor Elizabeth Hester
Senior Designer Tai Blanche
Managing Art Editor Michelle Baxter
Art Director Dirk Kaufman
Publishing Director Beth Sutinis
Production Ivor Parker
DTP Design Kathy Farias

DOWNTOWN BOOKWORKS INC.

PRODUCED BY DOWNTOWN BOOKWORKS INC.
President Julie Merberg
Director Patty Brown
Editor Sarah Parvis
DESIGNED BY GEORGIA RUCKER DESIGN
Designer and Illustrator Georgia Rucker

First published in Great Britain in 2006 by
Dorling Kindersley Limited,
80 Strand, London, WC2R 0RL
A Penguin Company

06 07 08 10 9 8 7 6 5 4 3 2 1

A CIP catalogue record for this book is available
from the British Library.

ISBN-13 978-1-40531-670-5
ISBN-10 1-40531-670-5

Colour reproduction by Colourscan, Singapore
Printed in China by Leo Paper Group

Discover more at
www.dk.com

Contents

What's Your Style Profile?

Are you chic and sleek or proud to be girly? Choose the answer that best describes you.

1 On non-uniform day at school, you plan on wearing:
- **a.** your new designer jeans.
- **b.** a simple sundress and lots of beaded necklaces.
- **c.** something sporty and casual.
- **d.** a polo shirt and khaki skirt.

2 You wouldn't be caught dead:
- **a.** with last season's handbag.
- **b.** in boring colours.
- **c.** wearing a frilly dress.
- **d.** in anything too bright.

3 You can never have enough:
- **a.** pairs of sunglasses.
- **b.** funky, chunky jewelry.
- **c.** trainers.
- **d.** cute skirts.

4 Your accessories are:
- **a.** Sparkly and trendy.
- **b.** Chunky and funky.
- **c.** You don't wear many.
- **d.** Simple and tasteful.

5 You usually wear your hair:
- **a.** long and poker straight.
- **b.** free and flowing or with lots of loose plaits.
- **c.** in a ponytail.
- **d.** fastened back with a headband or tortoiseshell clip.

6

6 Your bedroom is full of:

a. posters, pictures and slogans that you have ripped out of fashion magazines.

b. sweet smelling candles and lots of comfy floor cushions.

c. certificates and trophies you've won.

d. framed photographs of you and your friends.

7 Your grandma gives you money for your birthday. You spend it on:

a. clothes and shoes.

b. a vintage camera.

c. an iPod.

d. a new tennis racket.

8 When it comes to make up, you:

a. love to experiment with shimmery shadows.

b. own lots of fruity lip glosses.

c. aren't really interested at all.

d. limit your use to a subtle lipstick that perfectly matches your colouring.

ANSWERS

Mostly A's
Designer Diva

You love fashion and are all about whatever is hot right now. Nothing made you happier than playing dress up as a little girl and you'd spend all of your money on clothes if you could. You're into jeans, sparkly tops and great shoes.

Mostly B's
Boho Baby

You've got a unique funky style. You'll spend hours looking through your mum's wardrobe for cool scarves, beads and worn-in jeans. You don't care about trends and prefer to create your own look.

Mostly C's
Sporty Sister

You lead an active lifestyle and your clothes reflect that. Lots of sleek trainers and comfortable jeans and t-shirts. You don't like to spend a lot of time fussing over your appearance.

Mostly D's
Classic Cutie

You're all about crisp shirts and pressed skirts in simple styles and patterns. Occasionally, you'll buy a trendy bag to change things, but for the most part you prefer clothes that you can wear from year to year.

Are You Superstitious?

Do four-leaf clovers bring good fortune? Find out just how deeply you believe.

1 As you're changing into your kit for a big football game, you realise you forgot your lucky socks. You've never played a game without them. You:

a. completely freak out. You're doomed to miss every shot now!

b. call your mum to see if she can bring the socks to you.

c. shrug it off. It's your perfect passing skills that make you great on the field.

2 A black cat crosses your path. You:

a. bend down to pet him.

b. spend the rest of the afternoon waiting for something lucky to happen.

c. don't even notice.

3 Rumour has it you got the lead in the school play. You:

a. tell your best friend but ask her to keep quiet.

b. are secretly ecstatic but don't breathe a word until the official cast list goes up. You don't want to jinx it.

c. immediately start practising your lines.

4 Have you ever held an umbrella over your head indoors?

a. Yes

b. Probably, though you can't recall

c. Absolutely not — that's bad luck!

5 You are shopping in a book shop and there is a ladder leaning in your path. You:

a. ask someone to pass you the book you want.

b. walk several aisles away, just to avoid stepping under it.

c. stroll right over and grab the novel you have your eye on.

6 Your aunt tells you that it's bad luck to pick up a penny that's heads down. Later, you spot one on the ground. You:

a. are tempted to pocket it, but can't get your aunt's warning out of your mind.

b. pick it up anyway. Money's money.

c. avoid it at all costs.

O, Romeo!

7 In your dream last night, you saw your friend Amanda sobbing and upset. When you wake up in the morning, you:

a. immediately call her to make sure she's OK.

b. look for a dream book in the school library. You're curious about what your subconscious was trying to tell you.

c. vaguely remember that you had a nightmare, but shake it off. It was just a bad dream.

8 You have a dream catcher in your room because:

a. you think it looks really cool.

b. your best friend gave it to you and they're supposed to bring good fortune.

c. you've heard they ward off evil spirits.

9 At the park, a ladybird crawls on you. You

a. gently brush it off.

b. believe that you'll have good luck for the rest of the day.

c. start screaming. You hate bugs!

10 You've had the worst day ever and when you look at the calendar you realise it's Friday the 13th. You:

a. tell yourself it's just a coincidence.

b. aren't surprised. Nothing good ever happens on Friday the 13th!

c. think that could be why your day's been so awful.

ANSWERS

1 a=3 b=2 c=1
2 a=1 b=3 c=2
3 a=2 b=3 c=1
4 a=1 b=2 c=3
5 a=2 b=3 c=1
6 a=2 b=1 c=3
7 a=3 b=2 c=1
8 a=1 b=2 c=3
9 a=2 b=3 c=1
10 a=1 b=3 c=2

24–30 points
Legend Has It

It's hard to believe that you'll ever have bad luck, since you're taking so many steps to avoid it! While being a little superstitious is fine, don't let it take over your life. Remember: it's okay to hang out with friends when there's a full moon or even adopt a black cat.

17–23 points
Slightly Supernatural

While you think old wives' tales are kind of cool (you can't help but hold your breath every time you pass by a graveyard) you don't put too much stock in them. You are open-minded but know how to separate fact from fiction.

10–16 points
Superstition Shmooperstition

You don't have a superstitious bone in your body. You step on cracks, walk under ladders and use umbrellas indoors. Try not to judge other people who are believers. If knocking on wood makes them feel better, so be it.

If You Had A Million Pounds...

What would you do with all that money?

1 **How much of it would you give to charity?**

  a. Half

  b. £100,000

  c. None

2 **The first thing you'd buy would be:**

  a. a bigger house for your mum and dad.

  b. tonnes of books for the town library.

  c. a whole new wardrobe.

3 **Would you give any money to your friends?**

  a. Maybe, but probably only your best friend

  b. Definitely, you'd divide it up equally among them

  c. No way – mixing friendships and money is never a good idea.

4 **Where would you travel?**

  a. France. You'd love to see the Eiffel Tower and the Louvre.

  b. A developing nation, perhaps in Africa, where you could help people at the same time.

  c. Los Angeles. To visit Hollywood and go shopping on Rodeo Drive.

5 **The one thing you'd never live without is:**

  a. cash in your pocket at all times.

  b. a comfortable bed.

  c. designer sunglasses.

6 **The car you'd drive:**

  a. would definitely be nice, but not too flashy.

  b. would be small and environmentally friendly.

  c. would be a top-of-the-range convertible with leather seats and an amazing sound system.

7 You'd invest in:

a. stocks and shares.

b. art.

c. a brand new water park (named after you, of course!)

8 Now that money's no object you'd never miss:

a. the chance to travel and learn about anything that interests you.

b. a chance to give back to the world.

c. a private sale at your favourite shop.

ANSWERS

Mostly A's
Pretty Practical

You're responsible with money and though you'd definitely have fun with your cash, you'd also put aside a good chunk to make it last for a long, long time.

Mostly B's
Determined Do-Gooder

You're very conscious of how lucky you are and want to share your good fortune with other people. You just wouldn't feel right if you kept all the money for yourself, so you would use it to help out people who aren't as lucky as you.

Mostly C's
Serious Shopper

If you suddenly had money, you'd go wild, buying anything and everything that struck your fancy. Sharing and saving just wouldn't be in your plans.

Are You A Girly Girl?

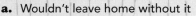

1. When choosing a lip gloss, you go for:

a. a shimmery pink that makes your lips look lush.

b. a fruity flavor like strawberry or mango.

c. one that keeps your lips from chapping.

2. When you get dressed for school in the morning, you:

a. make sure that your shoes, shirt and hair clips match.

b. want to look trendy, yet nice.

c. throw on something you feel comfortable and warm in.

3. The last time you got dirty was:

a. when you were five.

b. the other day when you helped your mum plant petunias.

c. during hockey practice.

4. How often do you wear nail polish?

a. Wouldn't leave home without it

b. On special occasions

c. Um, never

5. Your grandma buys you a pleated skirt and a pair of cords for your birthday. You return:

a. the cords.

b. neither. You love to be versatile.

c. the skirt. You hate showing off your legs.

6. When you pass notes to your friends, you:

a. always use a glitter pen.

b. fold the paper into impossibly small squares.

c. …you don't write notes.

Answers

Mostly A's
Feminine and Fabulous

If it's frilly, flirty or flashy, you're into it. You love pretty things and always want to look good. Pinks and purples are your favorite colours.

Mostly B's
Simple and Sweet

You're more of a classic beauty. You definitely care about your appearance but you're not obsessed with it. Green is a great hue for you.

Mostly C's
Cool and Casual

Outward appearances don't mean that much to you. Your clothes serve a function – to keep you covered. While you like to look nice, you don't try too hard. You favour greys and blues.

What Do Your **Doodles** Mean?

You may think scribbling absently in your notebook is just a way to pass the time, but your sketches could reveal something about you. Draw a picture of a house in the space below and include everything that makes you think of home.

▶▶ **Does the roof have tiles?** If so, you love to fantasise about the future and all of the wonderful things that'll be yours.

▶▶ **Did you draw a pathway** leading to your home? The path shows that you are a warm, welcoming person and that you love having visitors.

▶▶ **And trees?** If your house has lots of trees around it, you are a very optimistic person. If the trees are full of leaves, you are a social person who usually connects easily with others.

▶▶ **Are there people in your picture?** If they are stick figures, you like things to be very simple and do not usually get stressed out about details.

▶▶ **Are there cars?** This could symbolise that you have a busy family, with many people coming or going from the house.

▶▶ **What about flowers?** Drawing flowers and plants means you're a sweet, sensitive person who often thinks about the future in a positive way.

▶▶ **Does your house have a chimney?** If there is smoke coming out of that chimney, you're probably a happy person.

▶▶ **How about windows?** If you drew a house without windows, you are sad about something going on in your family. Big windows show that you have no secrets. You love to confide in others. If you drew curtains, you are a private person. You don't always like people to know what you are thinking.

13

WHAT KIND OF GUY
Do You Go For?

A clever clogs or sporting hero?
See what your answers reveal.

1 Your crush walked into class today wearing:

   a. his football shirt.

   b. a shirt and cords.

   c. a t-shirt with his favourite band's logo on it.

   d. new trainers that aren't even in shops yet.

2 In his spare time, he likes to:

   a. work on his jump shot.

   b. read as many books as he can.

   c. paint.

   d. hang out with his friends.

3 In order for you to like a guy, he must:

   a. love the outdoors as much as you do.

   b. get good marks in school.

   c. practically live at the cinema.

   d. be in the popular crowd at school.

4 Your dream boy wears his hair:

   a. very short.

   b. neatly trimmed.

   c. long and shaggy.

   d. short and spiky.

5 To you, a guy's most important quality is:

   a. a sense of humour.

   b. intelligence.

   c. thoughtfulness.

   d. his looks.

6 You'd lose interest if he:

   a. turned into a couch potato.

   b. tried to copy your work.

   c. made plans to meet you after school and didn't show up.

   d. was a terrible kisser.

7 In science class, your teacher asks that all lab partners include a guy and a girl. You pick:

a. the guy who you think is equally as smart as you. That way you can help each other.

b. the guy with the highest marks in the class.

c. the guy who doodles in his notebook for most of the lesson. He'll need your expertise.

d. the guy who sits in the back of the room making wisecracks and playing pranks on the teacher. At least your study sessions won't be boring.

8 School's over for the day and you want to accidentally bump into him. The first place you look is:

a. the football pitch.

b. the science labs.

c. the drama club meeting room.

d. on the benches outside with a group of his friends.

ANSWERS

Mostly A's
AWESOME ATHLETE
Cheering him on from the stands or challenging him to a tennis match is your idea of fun. In order for you to be interested in a boy, he's got to be into sport.

Mostly B's
BRAINS OVER BRAWN
You'll take the class president over the clown any day. You think being clever and sure of yourself is super cute. And you know you'll have lots to talk about.

Mostly C's
ARTSY FARTSY
If he can write you a poem or sing you a song, he'll have won you over. You like guys who are sensitive and caring. You can always tell what he's thinking.

Mostly D's
PRETTY AND POPULAR
If he's not the cutest, most well-liked boy in the class, you're not interested. You love to have fun and want to rule the school along with him.

How BLUNT Are You?

Sometimes being honest can hurt.
Do you tell it like it is or cushion the blow?

1 Your sister cut her hair really short and you think it looks awful. When she asks your opinion, you:

a. lie and tell her she looks great. You don't want to crush her.

b. say that you always wondered what she'd look like as a boy. Now you know.

c. admit that it's a big change, but after a few weeks you'll probably love it.

2 Your friend is trying out for the school chorus—even though she can't sing. When she belts out her audition song for you, you:

a. cover your ears. She sounds like a wounded animal!

b. suggest that she try a tune that doesn't require her to hold the end note for so long.

c. gently tell her that since she's such a fast runner, maybe the track team is more her speed.

3 Your mom bought you a frilly, pink dress to wear to your cousin's wedding. When she asks you if you like it, you:

a. force a smile and tell her she's the best.

b. say that you love the dress, but ask if it comes in a less puffy style.

c. tell her that you've always wanted to look like a stick of cotton candy.

4 When asked your opinion, you often:

a. think about how to phrase your answer. You don't want to hurt anyone's feelings.

b. tell them what you think they want to hear.

c. say the first thing that pops into your mind. Hey, the truth hurts.

5 You think your best quality is:

a. your kindness.

b. your fairness.

c. your ability to always think of a snappy comeback.

6 You get invited to a birthday party for a classmate that you don't like. You say:

a. "Are you kidding me? I'd rather stay home and rearrange my sock drawer."

b. "I'm sorry, but I already have plans that afternoon."

c. "Wouldn't miss it. Thanks for including me."

7 It's your dad's night to cook dinner and he's a mess in the kitchen. When he serves you up a plate of his "turkey surprise," you:

a. thank him for his hard work. He really slaved away to make this meal.

b. suggest that he add more salt next time.

c. ask if you can order takeout. Does he really expect you to eat this garbage?!

8 Your little brother has to get braces but he's afraid he's going to look really ugly with them. When he complains, you:

a. agree. Braces are really unattractive.

b. reassure him that he'll only have to wear them for a year or two and his teeth will look amazing when they come off.

c. tell him that he'll probably hate the way they look, but that plenty of people his age have them too, so it is not that big a deal.

9 At a sleepover, one of your friends confides that she has a crush on a guy who's kind of nerdy. You:

a. tell her to go for it. He'll definitely like her since she's so much more popular than he is.

b. declare that going out with him would be a social disaster. Hello, he's a dork!

c. comment on what a cute couple they'd make.

ANSWERS

1 a=1, b=3, c=2
2 a=3, b=2, c=1
3 a=1, b=2, c=3
4 a=2, c=1, b=3
5 a=1, b=2, c=3
6 a=3, b=2, c=1
7 a=1, b=2, c=3
8 a=3, b=1, c=2
9 a=2, b=3, c=1

TOTALLY DIPLOMATIC 14-20 points
You're a big believer in truth-telling, only you often think before you let loose. That way, your friends still get your point, but they aren't offended by it. You're a true diva of diplomacy.

STRAIGHT TO THE POINT 21-27 points
You certainly are direct! You definitely tell it like is, whether it makes people feel bad or not. While honesty is a great thing, being totally truthful isn't the best policy if it hurts someone's self esteem. Try softening your words sometimes. People will still get the message.

CAN'T HANDLE THE TRUTH 7-13 points
You're super nice and would almost rather lie than tell people something that might hurt them. Because of this, your friends appreciate your gentle nature. But don't let that cloud your judgment. If you don't agree with others or have a differing opinion, it's okay to speak up. Plus, if you had spinach stuck in your teeth, you would rather hear it from a friend, right?

What Kind of Person Will You Marry?

Will the man of your dreams be sentimental or self-assured? Witty or wise? See which type of guy you're most suited to.

1 You'd rather have:

a. a husband who made a lot of money, but worked long hours.

b. a husband who had lots of time to devote to you, but earned little money.

c. you don't care. As long as his work makes him happy and he loves you, you'll be the picture of marital bliss.

2 You'll meet your husband:

a. while summering in the South of France.

b. while you are volunteering for a local non-profit.

c. when mutual friends set the two of you up.

3 When he proposes it'll be:

a. on New Year's Eve at the stroke of midnight.

b. on a hike through the mountains just as the sun is setting.

c. when you least expect it.

4 Your wedding will be:

a. a huge evening affair with tons of guests, flowers, and a beautiful white gown.

b. a small gathering with just close family and friends.

c. filled with personal touches like photos of the two of you and handwritten vows.

5 Your dream honeymoon would be:

a. traveling through Europe.

b. an African safari.

c. swimming along the beach in the South Pacific.

6 You'll live:

a. in a high rise in a major city.

b. on a sprawling ranch with lots of animals and land.

c. in a cozy home with tons of pictures and candles.

7 If you have a fight, you'll:

a. scream and yell at each other until you collapse in laughter. You're both really intense.

b. both let the other one speak. Communication is really important.

c. both apologize for anything hurtful you may have said and vow to work it out before bedtime. Your parents always said, "Never go to sleep angry."

8 On weekends you'll often:

a. host cocktail parties.

b. explore a new museum, outdoor market, or hiking trail.

c. have a quiet dinner for two, by the fireplace.

9 Before you have kids, you'll:

a. start a college fund for them.

b. backpack around the world.

c. Kids, what kids?

10 When it comes to decisions about your kids:

a. it'll be mostly up to you. As their mother, you'll be more involved in their day-to-day lives.

b. he'll be the disciplinarian.

c. you'll both have equal input.

Answers

Mostly A's
DEBONAIR PAIR
You are destined for a jet-setting hubby who likes to live large. You're all about having a glamorous life filled with fancy things, a nice house, and a luxury car. Your guy will make sure you have everything you wish for and you will be the queen of your domain.

Mostly B's
DOWN TO EARTH DUO
It is important to you to have a solid partnership where you work through things openly. You may not be living in the lap of luxury, but you will build a life together and have just as much fun taking a walk as enjoying a fancy trip to Europe.

Mostly C's
REAL ROMANTICS
This guy never lets you forget how much you are loved. You're as close now as the day you fell in love and you constantly do nice things for one another. While you both hope to be successful, having the love and support of such a sweet and thoughtful partner is more than enough for you.

What Kind of FRIEND Are You?

Trusty and true? Or Needy Nelly?
Follow the arrows to find out!

START

Your best friend just had a huge fight with her parents. When she calls you sobbing, you:

tell her you're sorry and then explain what an awful day you've had.

gather the rest of your friends for a sleepover in her honour filled with silly movies and lots of popcorn.

spend hours consoling her over the phone, even though you have lots of homework to do.

In order to be your friend a person must be:

a good listener.

a ton of fun.

There's only one spot left on the cheerleading team and both you and a close friend want it. You:

call her and pretend to be the coach letting her know that tryouts have been rescheduled. She can't beat you if she isn't there.

put up a good fight. May the best girl win!

take yourself out of the running. You kind of like swimming better anyway.

Your friends often call you when they need someone to talk to.

At lunch you often sit with:

whoever you bump into first. You get along well with your entire class.

the same three girls everyday.

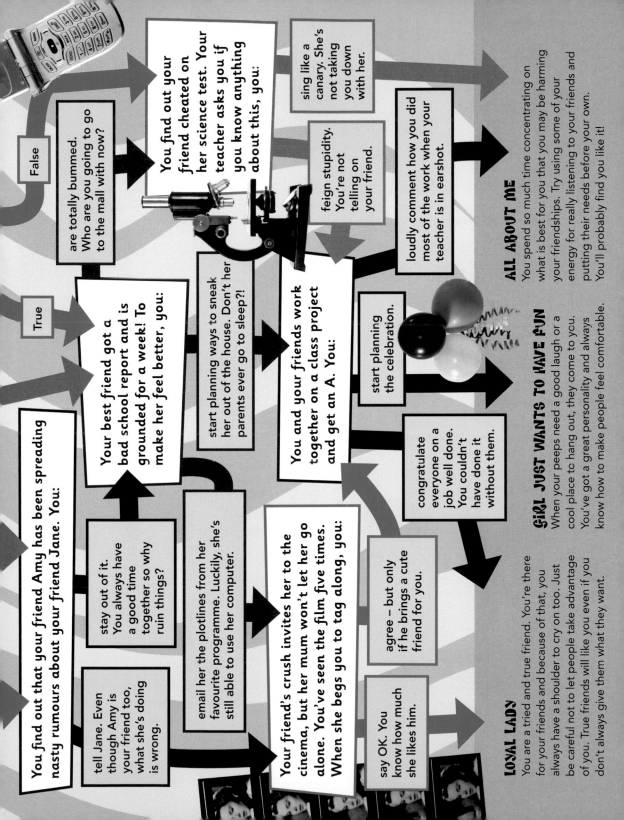

False

True

You find out that your friend Amy has been spreading nasty rumours about your friend Jane. You:

tell Jane. Even though Amy is your friend too, what she's doing is wrong.

stay out of it. You always have a good time together so why ruin things?

are totally bummed. Who are you going to go to the mall with now?

You find out your friend cheated on her science test. Your teacher asks you if you know anything about this, you:

sing like a canary. She's not taking you down with her.

feign stupidity. You're not telling on your friend.

loudly comment how you did most of the work when your teacher is in earshot.

Your best friend got a bad school report and is grounded for a week! To make her feel better, you:

start planning ways to sneak her out of the house. Don't her parents ever go to sleep?!

email her the plotlines from her favourite programme. Luckily, she's still able to use her computer.

You and your friends work together on a class project and get an A. You:

start planning the celebration.

congratulate everyone on a job well done. You couldn't have done it without them.

Your friend's crush invites her to the cinema, but her mum won't let her go alone. You've seen the film five times. When she begs you to tag along, you:

say OK. You know how much she likes him.

agree – but only if he brings a cute friend for you.

ALL ABOUT ME

You spend so much time concentrating on what is best for you that you may be harming your friendships. Try using some of your energy for really listening to your friends and putting their needs before your own. You'll probably find you like it!

GiRL JUST WANTS TO HAVE FUN

When your peeps need a good laugh or a cool place to hang out, they come to you. You've got a great personality and always know how to make people feel comfortable.

LOYAL LADY

You are a tried and true friend. You're there for your friends and because of that, you always have a shoulder to cry on too. Just be careful not to let people take advantage of you. True friends will like you even if you don't always give them what they want.

Do You Need *A New Look?*

Are you stuck in a style rut?
See if your fashion flair needs a tune-up.

1 **You've had the same hairstyle for:**

a. most of your life.

b. the last year or so.

c. the past week. You love to change things.

2 **When deciding what shoes to wear with an outfit, it's:**

a. torture. You've got a wardrobe full of footwear.

b. a decision. Do you want to be comfy or trendy?

c. no problem. You wear the same pair most days.

3 **You carry your books in:**

a. your arms.

b. a bag that is the right size for all of your school stuff.

c. a really cute satchel.

4 **When you look in your wardrobe, you see:**

a. lots of cutting-edge clothes like the ones in magazines.

b. a mixture of muted tones and flashier pieces for going out.

c. a series of light shirts and dark trousers that are easily matched.

5 **For you, bunches are:**

a. strictly for little girls.

b. an easy way to keep your hair out of your face.

c. cool, but only if they're worn low and loose.

6 The new trend is wearing big furry boots to school. You:

a. ignore it. You've never been one for following silly trends.

b. buy a pair but don't wear them every day.

c. live in yours.

8 At sleepovers, you usually wear:

a. a vest top and shorts.

b. a comfy old t-shirt that you've slept in for years.

c. a nightdress.

7 Your mum caught a glimpse of your outfit this morning and said:

a. "That skirt is way too short."

b. "Didn't you wear that yesterday?"

c. "I love that sweater on you."

Answers

1 a=3 b=2 c=1
2 c=1 b=2 c=3
3 a=2 b=3 c=1
4 a=1 b=2 c=3
5 a=1 b=3 c=2
6 a=3 b=1 c=2
7 a=1 b=3 c=2
8 a=2 b=3 c=1

19–24 points
Spice Things Up

If you look back at pictures of yourself over the years, they'd all look exactly the same no matter what age you were. You don't have to completely change overnight but you can make subtle moves. If you always wear your hair tied back, try letting it flow long and loose. Or put on a pastel top instead of your usual white. Change is good.

14–18 points
Happy With Who You Are

You definitely love to play around with trendy clothes and hairstyles but you also know what looks best on you. You're not going to veer too far away from your natural style. It's your signature look.

8–13 points
Trend Queen

You change your look so often your teachers can barely keep up with you! You're open to new ideas and love to experiment. You are still trying to figure out who you want to be. Keep note of the styles and cuts that look best on you to create your own classic look.

Does Your **Room** Reflect **who** You Are?

Is your décor a bore? Or does it showcase your personality perfectly?

1 Your dad let you paint your room lavender last year. Today you:

a. are so over it. What were you thinking?

b. still love it. It's such a soothing colour.

c. like it, but are thinking about asking if you can paint one wall a darker shade of purple for contrast.

2 The duvet cover on your bed was picked out by:

a. you and your friend.

b. you.

c. your mum.

3 Look at your walls. What's on them?

a. shots of your new favourite band.

b. a painting that your parents hung when you were little.

c. photos of family and friends and a couple of wall decorations that both you and your mum like.

4 You're a total tech junkie. In your room, you have:

a. a laptop, video games and a TV.

b. a great sound system.

c. no electronics. There's no room.

5 Your sister goes off to college, and your parents give you the option of moving into her much bigger room. You:

a. take it, but bring most of the stuff from your old room. You really like the vibe you've got going.

b. thank them but say that you're staying put. The space you have is perfect for you.

c. start moving in before your sis is even out of the door. Wonder if they'll let you get new furniture too?

6 When you have friends over, you mainly hang out:

a. in the living room. You prefer to keep your room private.

b. sometimes in the kitchen, sometimes in your bedroom.

c. in your bedroom. It's so cosy in there.

8 **If you could change one thing about your room, you'd:**

  a. have a walk-in wardrobe.

  b. get a new rug.

  c. junk everything and start from scratch.

9 **When you look around your room, you think:**

  a. everything in here is a true reflection of the person I am right now.

  b. is it too dark in here?

  c. this is a great room – for a nine year old.

7 **How many dolls or stuffed animals are in your room?**

  a. None. You stopped playing with them years ago.

  b. One or two. They're your favourites and you can't part with them.

  c. A tonne. You haven't gotten around to packing them away.

10 **You've had your current bed:**

  a. for about a year.

  b. since you moved out of the crib.

  c. you can't recall, although it's the most comfortable place in the world.

ANSWERS

1	a=1	b=3 c=2
2	a=2	b=3 c=1
3	a=3	b=1 c=2
4	a=3	b=2 c=1
5	a=2	b=3 c=1
6	a=1	b=2 c=2
7	a=3	b=2 c=1
8	a=2	b=3 c=1
9	a=3	b=2 c=1
10	a=2	b=1 c=3

24–30 points

Mirror Image

A stranger could walk into your room and instantly tell what kind of person you are. Every little detail – from the knick knacks on the wall to the rug on the floor – is perfectly suited to you.

17–23 points

Work In Progress

You like your room, but you're still working on getting it just right. A few tweaks here and there and soon it will be the ultimate haven for you and your friends.

10–16 points

Completely Outdated

You're growing up, but unfortunately your bedroom hasn't quite caught on yet. Try adding a few subtle accents, like floor cushions or well-placed mirrors. Ask your parents if there's any chance of repainting (and offer to help!). You'd be surprised at what a fresh coat of colour can do.

If You RULED THE WORLD...

With so many problems in the world, being a leader is a tough business. If you had the power, what would be your priority?

1 Everyone would live in a/an _____ house.
a. solar powered
b. equal sized
c. self-cleaning

2 People would be required to _____.
a. recycle
b. give a portion of their income to the less fortunate
c. take an ice cream break every day

3 Going to work would be _____.
a. optional
b. about more than just about money
c. way more fun

4 How many days a week would kids have to go to school?
a. Five. That's a good system.
b. Three, but the other two weekdays would be for volunteering
c. Four. People would be happier if they always had a three-day weekend.

5 You'd declare a day of appreciation for _____.
a. the environment
b. teachers
c. women

6 _____ would be banned forever.

  a. Littering
  b. Greed
  c. Stress

8 No one would have to _____ ever again.

  a. travel far to find a beautiful outdoor space
  b. struggle to feed their families
  c. settle for less than they deserve

9 Everyone would drive _____.

  a. a hybrid car
  b. a safe car
  c. . . . nothing. They could snap their fingers and be instantly transported wherever they wanted to go

7 _____ would be free for everyone.

  a. Travel
  b. Food
  c. Amusement parks

ANSWERS

Mostly A's

GREEN GIRL

If you were in charge, the environment would be your top priority. You'd make sure lakes were preserved, trees were planted and the air would be fresh and clean. Oh, and everyone would be required to spend part of each day outdoors!

Mostly B's

COMMUNITY CONSCIOUS

You want to knock out poverty once and for all. People would no longer worry about going hungry, affording an education, or having a secure retirement. Not one person in your world would want for anything.

Mostly C's

POSITIVELY IN CHARGE

You want everyone to just chill out and enjoy life. Everyone is too uptight and they'd be a lot more productive if relaxing were mandatory. You also want to make sure women are treated the same as men.

Does JEALOUSY Get The Better of You?

Are you genuinely happy for people or do you begrudge them their good fortune?

1 Your best friend is friendly with another girl in your class. The two of them have plans to hang out on Friday night. When they ask you if you want to join, you:

a. tell them you're busy, even though you're really not. You don't want to feel like the odd one out.

b. jump at the chance. If your friend gets on well with this girl, you probably will too.

c. ask if another friend can come as well – you have other friends too.

2 You ran for class president and lost. When the winner comes up to congratulate you on a great race, you:

a. commend her on a job well done. It was a fair fight.

b. turn your back. You should have won!

c. tell her that you're sad that you lost but you appreciate her kind words.

3 Jennifer's parents are very rich. Yours aren't nearly as well off. When she invites you to her enormous house, you:

a. say yes. She's an awesome girl.

b. decline. Being around her family just reminds you of everything you don't have.

c. wouldn't miss it. You hear she has a bowling alley in her basement!

4 Your older sister is popular, beautiful and super bright. When you look at her, you:

a. are proud to share her DNA.

b. wish you had flawless skin like her.

c. want to vomit. Really, who is that perfect?

5 You find out that your crush likes another girl. When you see her at school, you:

a. fight the urge to trip her.

b. secretly think that she looks like a horse.

c. smile brightly at her. Maybe if you became friends, it would bring you closer to him.

6 Your friend buys a dress that you've had your eye on for weeks. When she wears it to school, you:

a. tell her you're glad she got it. Now you can just borrow it from her.

b. say that pink really isn't her colour.

c. pretend not to notice. It's not worth fighting over.

8 You and your friend try out for the hockey team. She gets a spot but you don't. You:

a. refuse to speak to her.

b. give her a huge hug and ask if she can give you some pointers for next year.

c. start to cry and let her comfort you. You really wanted to play.

7 Your mum buys you a fake designer bag. Your archrival has the real thing. When she accidentally leaves it behind in the canteen, you:

a. immediately return it to her. You'd expect her to do the same for you.

b. think about switching it with yours, but quickly abandon that plan. You're not that mean.

c. leave it there. She should learn to be more careful with her things.

9 At dance practice, you get put in the back row while a much worse dancer is chosen to be front and centre. You:

a. ask to speak to the coach after practice. There must be some kind of mistake.

b. try to convince other members of the team to sign a petition saying that she should be moved.

c. try to concentrate on your routine. If you work hard enough, you'll earn a spot in the front row.

ANSWERS

1 a=3 c=1 b=2
2 a=1 b=3 c=2
3 a=1 b=3 c=2
4 a=1 b=2 c=3
5 a=3 b=2 c=1
6 a=2 b=3 c=1
7 a=1 b=2 c=3
8 a=3 b=1 c=2
9 a=2 b=3 c=1

22–27 points
Incredibly Envious

If someone has better clothes, more money than you or something you want, you can't help but hate them for it. The next time you feel yourself turning green with jealousy, try to focus on the positive things in your own life. You'll see that things aren't so bad after all.

16–21 points
Slightly Green

Your occasional case of jealousy can inspire you to strive for bigger and better things. As long as you are admiring the strong qualities of others and not just their stuff, your jealousy can be a healthy thing. Just don't let these feelings get the best of you.

9–15 points
Genuinely Grateful

You don't care about material possessions, so if someone has a more expensive outfit on than you do, then good for them. Kindness and loyalty are way more important than trying to get one up on your friends all the time.

Treasure It or Toss It?

Your room is so cluttered you can barely find your bed at night! The stuff you choose to hang on to can say a lot about you. If could only keep one item from each pair below, which would it be?

1
a. Your first pair of ballet shoes
b. Your comfy old pair of boots

2
a. A box of notes from your best friend
b. A stuffed animal you won at a fair when you were six

3
a. A camera that once belonged to your dad
b. Your favourite jumper, even though it has a hole in it

4
a. The first book you ever read
b. A stack of magazines with pictures of your favourite celebrities

5
a. Your first report card
b. Last year's school notebooks

6
a. Your karaoke machine, which may or may not work
b. The battery charger to an old mobile phone

7
  a. A baseball cap your crush gave you
  b. The cola can he drank out of one day at lunch

8
  a. A really old pair of shoes that still fit
  b. Mismatched socks

9
  a. A t-shirt you made in art class
  b. Your sister's old t-shirt that never fitted you

10
  a. The very first CD you ever bought
  b. All of your old CDs

Answers

Mostly A's

Sentimental Girl

Not all of your clutter is junk. Some of your stuff brings back memories and you don't want to let them go. You know how to separate the rubbish from the treasures. Now if only you could convince your mum to let you keep that karaoke machine!

Mostly B's

Clutter Bug

You can't seem to part with anything you've collected over the years. It all means something to you – from an old Halloween costume to a glitter pen with no cap. Having lots of stuff around you makes you feel safe. Once a month, try to part with something you don't need to keep clutter from taking over your life!

SAVER or SPENDER?

Do you save your pennies or does money burn a hole in your pocket? See what your answers say.

1 You're at the shops and see a pair of strappy sandals. You:

a. ask if they're available in your size.

b. check the price tag and then walk away. They are way out of your range.

2 Your favourite author has just written a new book. You:

a. rush out and buy a copy.

b. wait and read it at the library.

3 Your aunt gives you £20 for your birthday. What do you do with it?

a. Lots of songs online

b. Put it in the bank

4 You're running late for school and don't have time for breakfast. You:

a. buy food at school.

b. grab a piece of fruit and a cereal bar from the cupboard on the way out the door.

5 You get pocket money every week. So far, you've saved:

a. around £5. You just cleaned out your piggy bank for some adorable summer shirts.

b. £50. You're trying to save for a computer.

6 When will you get your first credit card?

a. As soon as your parents allow you to!

b. In your twenties. You see no reason to rush into something that could lead to debt.

7 On your way home from school, you see a beautiful bracelet in a shop window. You already have a million pieces of jewellery. You:

a. buy it anyway. You've got a party to go to this weekend and it'll look great.

b. ask the owner to put it on hold for you. Eventually you will have enough money to pay for it.

8 When it comes to money, your motto is:

a. "If you've got it, flaunt it."

b. "A penny saved is a penny earned."

9 You want a part-time job because:

a. you hate having to ask your parents for money.

b. you want to boost your savings.

10 You've asked your brother to borrow money:

a. once or twice, but it must have been for something really important.

b. never. If you can't pay for something yourself, you don't buy it.

ANSWERS

Mostly A's
GOTTA HAVE IT GIRL

You're an instant gratification kind of girl. When you see something you like, you buy it and worry about how you'll pay for it later. Try getting into the habit of spending half of your money and saving the other. Once you see your savings grow, it'll be worth it.

Mostly B's
SUPER SAVER

Thrifty is your middle name. You're really good at saving and realise that you don't really need everything you want. The idea of having a nice fat bank balance in the long run is more important to you.

33

Predict Your Friend's Future

Make copies of this quiz to pass around – or read the sentences aloud. Then fill in the blanks for both you and a pal. When you're done, swap sheets to compare how good a fortune teller you really are!

All About Me _____ (my name)

1. I _____ attend university.
      (will/will not)

2. I will drive a _____ .
              (type of car)

3. I will be a professional _____ .
                      (job)

4. I will get married when I'm _____ years old.
                      (age)

5. My husband will have _____ eyes
                  (colour)
   and _____ hair.
      (colour)

6. My husband will work as a _____ .
                      (job)

7. I would love to live in a _____
                      (type of house)
   in _____ .
      (town/city)

8. My family pet will be a _____
                      (type of animal)
   called _____ .

All About Her _____ (her name)

1. She _____ attend university.
      (will/will not)

2. She will drive a _____ .
                (type of car)

3. She will be a professional _____ .
                        (job)

4. She will get married when she's
   _____ years old.
   (age)

5. Her husband will have _____ eyes
                    (colour)
   and _____ hair.
      (colour)

6. Her husband will work
   as a _____ .
        (job)

7. She would love
   to live in _____
            (type of house)
   in _____ .
      (town/city)

8. Her family pet will be a _____ (type of animal) called _____.

9. She will have her first child when she is _____ (age) years old.

10. She will have _____ (number) children: _____ (number) girls and _____ (number) of boys.

11. During the summer, her kids will _____.

12. Her favourite hobby will be _____.

13. She will have lots of _____.

14. If she appeared on television, it would be because _____.

9. I will have my first child when I am _____ (age) years old.

10. I will have _____ (number) children: _____ (number) girls and _____ (number) of boys.

11. During the summer, my kids will _____.

12. My favourite hobby will be _____.

13. I will have lots of _____.

14. If I appear on television, it would be because _____.

Your Score

Now exchange papers. Give yourself one point for every correct match.

11–14 points
Super Psychic

Wow, you're totally in tune with your friend's hopes for the future. Now comes the fun part: seeing if your predictions come true!

6–10 points
Sort of Psychic

You're pretty good at seeing the future, but don't quit your day job! Then again, who knows what will happen in the next ten or twenty years. . .

0–5 points
Not So Psychic

Better luck next time. But look on the bright side – you can take the quiz again! You and your friend can agree to a rematch next year!

What Makes You Angry?

Do you let little things eat at you or does it take something major to get you cross? See where your temper lies.

1 You just found out that a friend has been flirting with the guy you're in love with – even though she knows you like him! You:

a. call her and ask her to explain herself. You don't want to get all worked up over something if it isn't true.

b. wait by her locker and when she arrives, have an argument. You are no longer friends.

c. are annoyed but don't confront her. I mean, it's not like he's your boyfriend or anything. And friends are more important than guys any day.

You'd be most upset if:

a. someone was talking about you behind your back.

b. you felt discriminated against.

c. you thought you were being lied to.

You get invited to a boy/girl sleepover and really want to go. When you ask your mum, she says no way. You:

a. don't ask again. You'd rather go on the class ski trip next month, and you have to choose your battles.

b. throw a tantrum and refuse to speak to her for a week. If your parents are going to treat you like a baby, then you'll act like one.

c. tell her you're disappointed and ask her why she won't let you go. Maybe if you understand her reasoning, you can get her to change her mind.

4 Your brother is at his most infuriating when he:

a. goes through your things. He's such a sneak!

b. simply breathes. Just being in the same room with him drives you crazy.

c. makes a comment about girls being weaker than boys.

5 A friend borrows your favourite shirt and spills tomato sauce all over it. When she tells you what happened, you:

a. let her know that this is the last time you'll ever lend her anything again.

b. agree to forgive her – if she bakes you a batch of her famous double chocolate chip cookies.

c. try not to get too angry. Accidents happen.

36

6 Your little sister constantly steals your CDs and never returns them. You:

a. start borrowing her things and "forgetting" to give them back.

b. put a lock on your door. You've got to keep her out somehow.

c. remind her yet again that you don't mind if she uses your stuff – just as long as she gives it back.

7 You'd be most likely to join:

a. the environmental club. You want to improve the planet.

b. the debate club. You love to argue.

c. the school newspaper. You want to expose injustice.

8 You study really hard for your English test and only get a B+. The girl who sits next to you gets an A, but you know that she cheated. What do you do?

a. What can you do? It's not like you have actual proof.

b. Tell your teacher. It's not fair! You worked really hard.

c. Let the girl know that you saw her cheating – and next time, you're not keeping quiet.

9 You'd really get angry if:

a. someone took your dinner money.

b. your favourite gadget mysteriously disappeared.

c. your house was broken into.

10 You ask the assistant at your favourite shop to put a pair of boots on hold for you. When you go back later to buy them, they've been sold to another customer. You:

a. demand to know what happened. You have a skirt they'd look perfect with.

b. take it as a sign that you weren't meant to own them.

c. shout that you'll never shop there again and then tell all of your friends to boycott the shop too.

Answers

1	a=2	b=3	c=1
2	a=3	b=1	c=2
3	a=1	b=3	c=2
4	a=2	b=3	c=1
5	a=3	b=2	c=1
6	a=2	b=3	c=1
7	a=1	b=3	c=2
8	a=1	b=3	c=2
9	a=1	b=2	c=3
10	a=2	b=1	c=3

Always Sweating the Small Stuff
24–30 points
It doesn't take much to irritate you. Instead of getting angry about things that you have little control over, try to focus your energies on what's going right in our life. You'll be a much happier person!

Slightly Steamed
17–23 points
You do get upset, but you try to think things through before totally freaking out. Occasionally, your temper will get the best of you. If someone wrongs you, you're sure to speak up about it. You are no pushover!

Slow Burner
10–16 points
You're extremely even-tempered and only allow yourself to get angry when you feel like you or someone you love is being treated unfairly. You don't let day-to-day drama upset you. It's just not worth it.

If You Were AN ANIMAL...

Furry or flying? Slippery or scampering? Which creature is most like you? See what your answers reveal.

1 If you had some free time, you'd love to spend it:

a. running in the park.

b. lounging on the sofa.

c. hanging out at the beach.

d. exploring a new place.

2 If someone walked into your room, the first thing they'd notice would probably be:

a. your big comfy bed.

b. how organised all of your stuff is.

c. your bright blue walls.

d. the posters on your ceiling.

3 Your daily beauty routine includes:

a. brushing your hair at least 100 times.

b. making sure your nails are neatly trimmed.

c. slathering on sweet smelling moisturizer.

d. splashing water on your face and running your fingers through your hair.

4 You have a lot of hobbies but your favourite is:

a. football.

b. ballet.

c. swimming.

d. gymnastics.

5 You love to sleep:

a. sprawled out in the middle of your bed.

b. curled up in a ball.

c. wrapped tightly in your covers.

d. on your stomach.

6 You don't like:

a. being yelled at.

b. getting messy.

c. cold weather.

d. people who invade your personal space.

7 You won't leave home without:

a. your beaded name necklace.

b. an elastic to hold your hair back.

c. sunglasses.

d. your music.

Mostly A's
COMPLETELY CANINE

You're most happy when you can spend the day running and playing, and then come home to a nice, fluffy bed – all the things that dogs love to do. You're especially likeable and have lots of friends.

Mostly B's
CURIOUS CATWOMAN

Delicate and graceful are the words that best describe you. You always look clean and fresh and are very aware of what's going on around you – although you don't always let people know what you're really thinking.

Mostly C's
LEAPING LIZARD

If the weather's warm and water is nearby, you're right at home. You love to feel the sunshine on your face as you take a leisurely nap outdoors. You are a patient and relaxed person with a disposition as sunny as your favourite places.

Mostly D's
BIRDS ON THE BRAIN

You're an adventurer at heart and would love to go skydiving or bungee jumping someday. (Obviously heights don't scare you!) Someday you want to travel to space so you can see what's beyond the sky.

8 If you could run away and join the circus, you'd love to be:

a. a clown.

b. an acrobat.

c. a magician.

d. a flying trapeze artist.

Are You a SNOB?

We all have our choosy moments, but are yours getting out of control? Follow these clues to see just how particular you can be.

When it comes to your classmates, you:

only hang out with a select group. You have an image to uphold.

fit in easily with people in several different groups, but steer clear of the younger classes.

are friendly with most of them, although there are a couple of people you don't care for.

You're at a friend's house for dinner. Frozen pizza is on the menu and it doesn't look too appetizing. You:

stick to the salad. You don't know how long that pizza has been frozen.

dig in. You are just glad it is dinnertime!

protest because she's a total nerd. You know she won't fit in with your friends and you don't want to deal with it.

On a class trip you share a seat with your best friend, who's reading a copy of a lame teen magazine. When she's done, she asks if you want to read it. You:

You made plans to go to a friend's party and your mum is forcing you to bring your shy cousin, who's visiting. You:

protest because she is really quiet and you don't want to babysit her all night.

hope that introducing her to your friends will bring her out of her shell a bit.

You're at the mall with your friends and they want to go into a shop that sells cheap, funky clothes. You:

wrinkle your nose. You don't wear that kind of clothing.

tag along with them. It's not really your style, but maybe you'll find something you like.

There's a new girl in school and rumour has it that her dad is in prison. When she asks to sit with you at lunch. You:

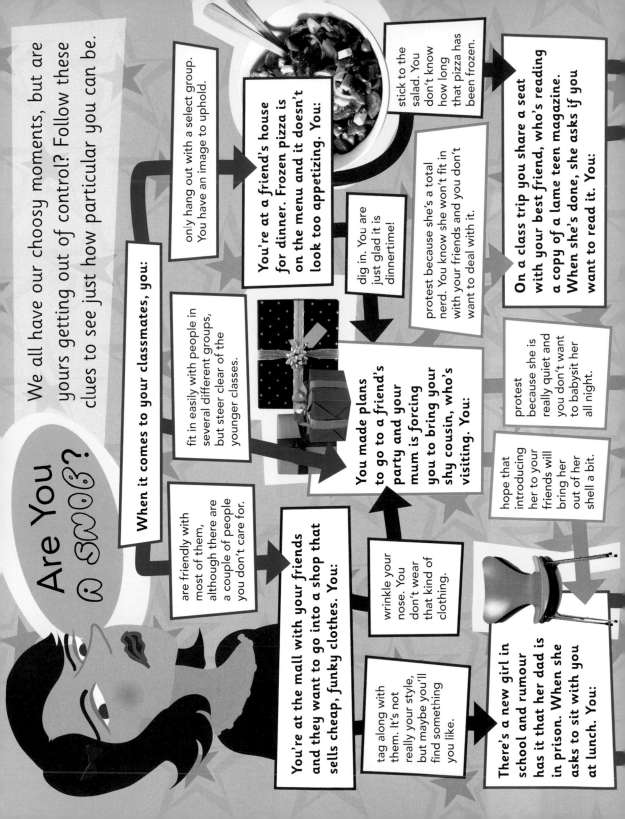

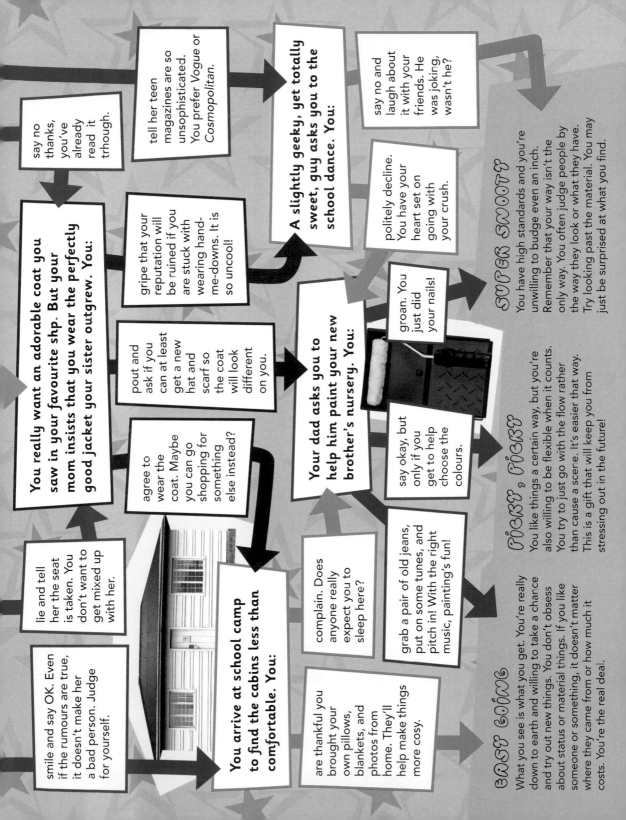

You really want an adorable coat you saw in your favourite shp. But your mom insists that you wear the perfectly good jacket your sister outgrew. You:

say no thanks, you've already read it trhough.

tell her teen magazines are so unsophisticated. You prefer *Vogue* or *Cosmopolitan*.

gripe that your reputation will be ruined if you are stuck with wearing hand-me-downs. It is so uncool!

pout and ask if you can at least get a new hat and scarf so the coat will look different on you.

agree to wear the coat. Maybe you can go shopping for something else instead?

A slightly geeky, get totally sweet, guy asks you to the school dance. You:

say no and laugh about it with your friends. He was joking, wasn't he?

politely decline. You have your heart set on going with your crush.

lie and tell her the seat is taken. You don't want to get mixed up with her.

smile and say OK. Even if the rumours are true, it doesn't make her a bad person. Judge for yourself.

Your dad asks you to help him paint your new brother's nursery. You:

groan. You just did your nails!

say okay, but only if you get to help choose the colours.

You arrive at school camp to find the cabins less than comfortable. You:

complain. Does anyone really expect you to sleep here?

grab a pair of old jeans, put on some tunes, and pitch in! With the right music, painting's fun!

are thankful you brought your own pillows, blankets, and photos from home. They'll help make things more cosy.

Which **Historical Figure** Would You Be?

There are many women throughout history who have changed the world. See which one of these distinguished dames you have the most in common with.

1 It's the weekend! Your plans include:

a. working on your science fair project. You think you have a good shot of winning a prize.

b. volunteering at your local soup kitchen for a few hours.

c. finishing up a short story you've been writing.

d. going for a hike. There's a new trail you want to explore.

2 When your parents ask you what you want for your birthday, you request:

a. a telescope.

b. a donation to your favourite charity.

c. a book token.

d. a mountain bike.

3 Your ultimate goal is to:

a. find a cure for cancer.

b. help the less fortunate.

c. go to a booksigning – of your own published work!

d. travel to the remote corners of the world.

4 Your favourite school subject is:

a. chemistry.

b. social studies.

c. English.

d. art.

5 Your favourite website is:

a. howstuffworks.com

b. redcross.org.uk

c. amazon.co.uk

d. nationalgeographic.co.uk

6 Your best friend is coming over to hang out. You'll probably:

a. bake cookies. You love to mix stuff together and see what comes out.

b. talk about organising a school fundraiser to raise money for victims of a natural disaster.

c. play Scrabble. You're the reigning champ and she's determined to beat you.

d. dye your hair pink. You're sick of your old look.

7 You can see your life and your work taking you to a location like:

a. France.

b. India.

c. England.

d. Kenya.

8 You're known for:

a. being able to figure out complex problems without stressing out.

b. your tremendous heart.

c. the funny poems you write for your friends on their birthdays.

d. your impulsiveness and sense of adventure.

ANSWERS

Mostly A's
Marie Curie
A brilliant scientist who discovered radioactivity, Marie Curie's work shaped the way we treat diseases today. Like her, you're determined to break new ground. You're smart, dedicated, and patient – all the markings of a successful pioneer.

Mostly B's
Mother Teresa
The patron saint of the poor, Mother Teresa helped thousands of people in her lifetime. You possess the same selflessness that she did and put the well-being of others first. You will do great things for the world.

Mostly C's
Jane Austen
Like this successful author, you want to write books that are not only entertaining, but send a message about society's treatment of women. With an imagination like yours, you'll go far. You will make your mark with your pen.

Mostly D's
Amelia Earhart
A true world traveller, you want to lead a life full of adventure, just like Amelia, who broke records for flight speed and distance and set out to fly around the globe in 1932. You won't be satisfied unless you're exploring new places and pushing yourself to new heights every day.

Is He Crushworthy?

You like a guy, but does he deserve such a fabulous female's attention?

1 You're hurrying to class when you trip and drop all of the books you were carrying. Just as you bend down to pick them up, your guy walks by. He:

a. stops to help you and then offers to walk you the rest of the way.

b. gives you a smile and a wink but keeps going.

c. doesn't even notice.

2 He often flirts with:

a. you – and every other girl in school.

b. you. It is so much fun!

c. no one. Come to think of it, you never see him talking to girls.

3 You have PE together and get put on the same volleyball team. As you're both going for the ball, you bump into each other and fall down. He:

a. immediately helps you up and asks if you're OK.

b. gives you an annoyed look as he brushes himself off.

c. mumbles an apology and then limps off the field.

4 You're in line behind him in the canteen and there's only one piece of chocolate cake left, which you both reach for. He:

a. steps back and lets you have it, without saying a word.

b. takes it.

c. reaches for it, but offers to share with you if you'll sit next to him.

5 You drag your friends to his football match, where he's the star striker. Afterwards, you congratulate him on a great game. He replies:

a. "Thanks for coming. Fan support is really important."

b. "Did you see that amazing goal I scored at the end of the game? That's why they call me the man!"

c. "Hey thanks! I'm starving. Do you want to grab a burger with me?"

6 You're having a lot of trouble with your maths homework and he's a whiz. When you ask him for help, he:

a. tells you that he's not a very good teacher, but he'll do what he can.

b. asks you to meet him in the library after school for a tutoring session.

c. apologises, but says he just doesn't have the time.

7 You run into him at the weekend when he's shopping with his mum. He:

a. nods hello and keeps walking.

b. introduces you to his mother.

c. doesn't notice you until you're practically standing in front of him.

8 On the school bus there's only one seat left – next to him. When you ask if you can sit down, he:

a. says OK, but that there are other seats on the bus.

b. moves his bag and asks if you have enough room.

c. doesn't hear you. He's wearing headphones and staring out the window.

9 You wish he:

a. would ask you out.

b. knew you were alive.

c. could stop referring to you as babe. You do have a name.

Answers

1 a=3 b=1 c=2
2 a=1 b=3 c=2
3 a=3 b=1 c=2
4 a=2 b=1 c=3
5 a=2 b=1 c=3
6 a=2 b=3 c=1
7 a=1 b=3 c=2
8 a=1 b=3 c=2
9 a=3 b=2 c=1

22–27 points
Worth It!

This guy is adorable! He's smart, sweet and would make a great boyfriend. Never pass up an opportunity to talk to him when you see him. Before you know it, he'll be asking you for a date.

16–21 points
Could Be Worth It

His failure to notice you doesn't mean he doesn't like you. He's just not used to the attention! Keep chatting him up and eventually he'll get the hint that you like him. No one's that clueless!

9–15 points
Totally Not Worth It

This guy's a loser. He only cares about himself and you definitely don't need someone like that in your life. You should be with a guy who can appreciate how smart and beautiful you really are!

Tried and True or Something New?

Every choice you make reveals something about the inner workings of your mind. Which item would you pick?

1 **You're at the ice cream shop. Of the 27 flavours, you pick:**

a. vanilla.

b. strawberry.

c. double peanut butter mocha chip.

2 **Taking a foreign language is a requirement at your school. You'd love to learn:**

a. French.

b. Russian.

c. Japanese.

3 **As a child, your favourite bedtime story was:**

a. *Cinderella*.

b. *Snow White*.

c. *Goldilocks and the Three Bears*.

4 **You are learning gymnastics and can master only one routine. You opt for:**

a. a floor exercise.

b. the balance beam.

c. the vault.

5 **You've got lots of hair accessories but you usually choose:**

a. the same brown tortoiseshell clips.

b. a hair band that matches your outfit.

c. one of your wild, brightly-printed head scarfs.

6 **For dinner, your friend's mother serves you an unfamiliar dish. When the platter of reddish, orange-ish goo arrives, you:**

a. grab bread and skip the mystery meal.

b. take a tiny portion to be polite.

c. fill up your plate and hope for the best.

answers

Mostly A's
STEADY AND SAFE

You know what you like and you stick to it, even if others around you are going off in different directions. You have a strong practical side and do not like to be put on the spot.

Mostly B's
CURIOUS YET CAUTIOUS

You are intrigued by fresh ideas, but like to weigh your options before jumping into new things. Both careful and fun, you are observant and take your time making decisions.

Mostly C's
UP FOR A CHALLENGE

When everyone else is going left, you turn right. Adventurous and impulsive, you love to do your own thing, even if it's not the most popular choice. And if there's a risk to be taken in the process, even better.

46

Will You Be FRIENDS FOREVER?

Is she a fair weather acquaintance or in it for the long haul?

2 You haven't seen her all summer because you were both on holiday. The minute you get home, you:

a. call and ask her to hang out. You have so many things to tell her.

b. send her a text message to let her know you're back.

c. email your holiday friends. You miss them already.

4 A girl you don't like invites your best friend over and tells her specifically not to bring you. Your friend:

a. doesn't go. You two are a package deal.

b. goes, but tells you later that she felt totally guilty about it the whole time.

c. hangs out with her. Just because you're best friends doesn't mean you have to do everything together.

1 Your friend is asked out by a guy she likes – for the same night as your birthday party, she:

a. tells him she's busy. She'd never ditch you on your special day.

b. invites him to the party. This way she can hang out with both of you.

c. promises to make it up to you and goes on the date. Have you seen how cute he is?!

3 Your dog passed away. She:

a. cries with you. She's known you for so long, it's like she lost a beloved pet too.

b. walks you to the pet store. Maybe a new puppy will make you feel better.

c. scribbles a note during English class.

5 Even though you're getting older, sometimes you still play with your dolls. She's outgrown them. When she finds you playing with them, she:

a. plays with you.

b. doesn't say anything.

c. makes fun of you for being such a little girl.

ANSWERS

Mostly A's
LIFELONG PALS

You guys have a special bond that nothing can break. Even if the future takes you in different directions, you'll always find a way to stay in touch and share your lives with one another. You are truly best friends.

Mostly B's
FRIENDS FOR NOW

You have a good time, but anything deeper than that may not be in the cards. Your friendship might end with high school. But when you're adults, you'll look back on your memories of the time you spent together and smile.

Mostly C's
CASUAL COHORT

She may be fun to hang with sometimes, but she's not very nice and not always loyal – the hallmarks of true sisterhood. You can still talk to her, but save your secrets for someone who is sure to keep them.

47

What is YOUR OUTLOOK?

We can't have everything we want, but there are some things we just can't live without. Pick one of each to reveal your outlook.

1 Your mum will only let you buy one pair of shoes this school year. You choose:

a. a pair of totally unique cowboy boots.

b. black boots that you can wear with everything.

2 It's important that your best friend:

a. have a lot in common with you.

b. be completely loyal.

3 You can't imagine a world without:

a. french fries.

b. flowers.

4 If your house was on fire and you only had time to grab one thing, it'd be:

a. your favourite necklace.

b. a family photo.

5 You have a crush on a boy at school because he's:

a. very sweet and handsome.

b. really clever and funny.

6 You have to add one class to your timetable, which do you pick?

a. Film studies

b. Business studies

7 If you could be famous or rich, but not both, which would you choose?

a. Fame

b. Money

8 A friend calls you crying just as you're about to go to the movies with your sister. You:

a. break your plans to come to her rescue.

b. tell her you are so sorry, but ask her if you can call her later.

9 You find £100 on the street. You:

a. hit the shops immediately.

b. save it. You really want a video mobile phone and now you're £100 closer to your goal.

10 This summer, you plan to:

a. work on your tan.

b. brush up on your Spanish.

11 You have an after-school job that you hate, but rely on for money. What do you do?

a. Quit. Life's too short to be unhappy.

b. Stick it out until something else crops up. It's a job after all.

ANSWERS

Mostly A's

RIGHT HERE, RIGHT NOW

You live in the moment. Your friends, your family, your hobbies – they are perfectly suited to who you are right this second. In fact, you can't imagine your life without them. You have trouble visualizing the future.

Mostly B's

WHAT'S NEXT?

You like to fantasize about where you'll be in five, ten, or twenty years, and the things you value reflect your forward-thinking. You can do without what's hot today because you're focusing on tomorrow.

How **Trustworthy** Are You?

When your conscience tells you
to do the right thing, do you listen?

1 Your friend Christie confides that she has a crush on a boy named Peter. She asks you not to tell anyone. You:

a. keep your lips sealed. A promise is a promise.

b. tell your friend Karen. Surely, Christie was going to tell her anyway right?

c. write an anonymous note to Peter letting him know that Christie likes him.

2 You accidentally see the answers to a big maths test on your teacher's desk. You:

a. swipe the test when she's not looking and make copies for your friends.

b. kindly let your teacher know that her exam is in full view.

c. take a glance at the section on long division before looking away – you're terrible at solving those equations.

3 You come home from school and overhear your mum gossiping on the phone to her best friend. You:

a. loudly announce, "Mom, I'm home," so she knows you're in the house.

b. think about listening in on her conversation but then abandon the idea. You'd hate it if your mom did that to you.

c. stand outside the door and eavesdrop. Maybe they'll say something about you!

4 When someone in your group of friends has big news, they often:

a. tell you first. They know you'll spread the word for them.

b. tell you first because they know you'll take whatever they say to the grave.

c. tell you when they see you.

5 You find out your sister's Instant Messenger password. You:

a. do nothing with the information. You have your own screenname. Why would you need to use hers?

b. frequently sign on to her account and pretend to be her.

c. log on as her one night after she "borrowed" your favourite jumper without your permission. But sign off immediately because you feel guilty.

6 You're in the ladies' toilets at the shopping centre, and the woman standing next to you at the sink accidentally leaves behind a gift voucher for your favourite store. You:

a. make a half-hearted attempt to find her and end up keeping the gift card for yourself.

b. chase her down and return the card.

c. pocket it. Finder's keepers.

Answers

1 a=3 b=2 c=1

2 a=1 b=2 c=3

3 a=1 b=3 c=2

4 a=3 b=1 c=2

5 a=2 b=3 c=1

6 a=2 b=3 c=1

0–6 points
Ethically Challenged

You definitely know right from wrong, but you always seem to make the choice that's best for you, without worrying about how your actions will affect others. Next time you're tempted to spill a secret or cheat on a test, ask yourself how your friends and family would feel if they knew what you were doing. Is hurting them really worth the risk?

7–12 points
Good at Heart

It's hard to be honest all of the time and you definitely feel tempted by secrets or gossip. But you have a strong conscience that is capable of pointing you in the right direction. Always listen to your inner voice.

13–18 points
Thoroughly Honest

You're a super trustworthy girl. Your friends know that they can always count on you to keep their secrets and make the right choices. Your loyalty and honesty are truly treasured qualities.

CITY SLICKER or COUNTRY CREATURE

Do you thrive in the great outdoors or is the thrill of the big city calling your name? Follow the clues to find out where you belong.

START

On your very first trip to New York City, you:

- begin studying a map. The subway system can't be too hard to figure out, right?
- can't decide whether to visit the Empire State Building or Central Park first.
- spend a lot of time in your hotel room. The crowds, dirt and chaos are so overwhelming.

Is being able to drive important to you?

No → **It's important to you to have:**

Yes →

In your garden you plan to grow:

- tomatoes, carrots, potatoes and anything else the garden centre sells.
- simple flowers like pansies or tulips.
- . . . garden? You can barely even keep the cactus in your room alive!

It's important to you to have:

great restaurants and funky boutiques nearby.

You've always imagined that you'd live in:

- a big house with a sprawling, green lawn.
- a flat with lots of windows for the sun to stream through.

A perfect vacation would include:

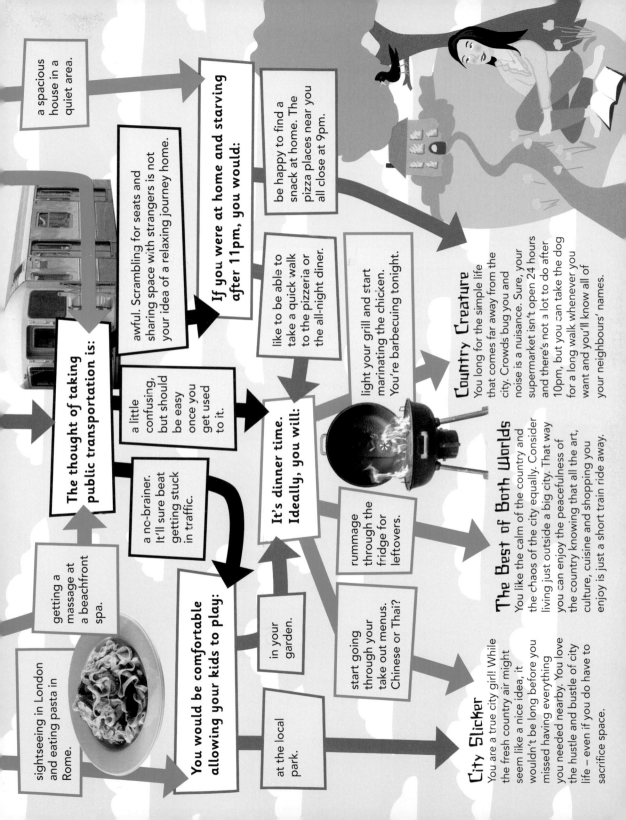

a spacious house in a quiet area.

The thought of taking public transportation is:

awful. Scrambling for seats and sharing space with strangers is not your idea of a relaxing journey home.

If you were at home and starving after 11pm, you would:

be happy to find a snack at home. The pizza places near you all close at 9pm.

like to be able to take a quick walk to the pizzeria or the all-night diner.

a little confusing, but should be easy once you get used to it.

light your grill and start marinating the chicken. You're barbecuing tonight.

Country Creature
You long for the simple life that comes far away from the city. Crowds bug you and noise is a nuisance. Sure, your supermarket isn't open 24 hours and there's not a lot to do after 10pm, but you can take the dog for a long walk whenever you want and you'll know all of your neighbours' names.

a no-brainer. It'll sure beat getting stuck in traffic.

It's dinner time. Ideally, you will:

sightseeing in London and eating pasta in Rome.

getting a massage at a beachfront spa.

You would be comfortable allowing your kids to play:

in your garden.

rummage through the fridge for leftovers.

The Best of Both Worlds
You like the calm of the country and the chaos of the city equally. Consider living just outside a big city. That way you can enjoy the peacefulness of the country knowing that all the art, culture, cuisine and shopping you enjoy is just a short train ride away.

start going through your take out menus. Chinese or Thai?

at the local park.

City Slicker
You are a true city girl! While the fresh country air might seem like a nice idea, it wouldn't be long before you missed having everything you needed nearby. You love the hustle and bustle of city life – even if you do have to sacrifice space.

What's Your NUMBER?

Numerology is the study of numbers
and how they relate to your life.
To find out what your Destiny Number means,
use the chart and instructions below.

1 Write down your full birth name in the space below.

YOUR NAME:

Eilidh   Joy (middle)   Maxwell (last)

2 Using the chart below, write down the number that corresponds to each
letter in your first name, then your middle name and finally your last name.

CORRESPONDING NUMBERS:

593948   167   4165533

3 Add up the numbers in each of your names. If the sums have two digits, then
add them together until you get a single digit. For example, if your name
was Julia, you would add up the numbers 1+3+3+9+1, for a sum of 17. Then
add 1+7 for a total of 8. Repeat this process for each of your names.

ADD UP THE NUMBERS:

11   5   9

4 Add the totals together until you get
a single digit, your Destiny Number.

5 Now, find your
number to see
what it says
about you!

ADD UP THE NUMBERS

NUMBERS CORRESPONDING TO
YOUR FIRST NAME: 11

NUMBERS CORRESPONDING TO
YOUR MIDDLE NAME: 5

NUMBERS CORRESPONDING TO
YOUR LAST NAME: 9

2 + 2 = 4

TOTAL FROM ALL NAMES: 25

NUMBER CHART

1 = A, J, S
2 = B, K, T
3 = C, L, U
4 = D, M, V
5 = E, N, W
6 = F, O, X
7 = G, P, Y
8 = H, Q, Z
9 = I, R

For example: ANNA JANE SMITH

ANNA would be 1+5+5+1=12.   **1+2 = 3**

JANE would be 1+1+5+5 =12.   **1+2 = 3**

SMITH would be 1+4+9+2+8=24.   **2+4 = 6**

Finally, add 3+3+6=12. 1+2=3.
Anna's destiny number would be **3**

WHAT DOES YOUR DESTINY NUMBER MEAN?

1 You are a natural-born leader and you like your freedom. Full of ambition and creativity, you hate it when people tell you what to do.

2 You're a very supportive, fair friend. You never take sides when people you love fight, and try really hard never to hurt anyone's feelings.

3 You love to have fun. You always look on the bright side of life. Your glass is always half full and people are drawn to your good cheer.

4 You're a serious person and you like to plan everything very carefully. You like to feel in control, but can also remain calm and collected if something goes wrong.

5 Adventure is the name of the game for you. You're always up for trying new things and can often convince your friends to do so too.

6 You're a cautious person. You tend to worry a lot. Always happy to entertain yourself, you may prefer watching movies or relaxing at home to going out.

7 You're a non-conformist and love to go your own way. When people take the time to get to know you, they see how intelligent and wonderfully unique you are.

8 You know exactly what you want and never have trouble making decisions. You're also attracted to money and hope to have lots of it someday.

9 You've got a heart of gold and want to help make the world a better place. You have a variety of talents and excel at everything you set out to do.

What's Your Dream job?

You've probably thought about what you want to do when you grow up, but is it really right for you? See which of these paths you're destined to follow.

1 **In PE, a friend accidentally gets hit in the face with a ball. You:**

   a. apply pressure to the wound and reassure her that everything's going to be okay.

   b. complain about how PE should really be outlawed. It's so dangerous!

   c. start interviewing the "witnesses" to the accident.

   d. offer to let her use your concealer to hide what's sure to be a major bruise.

2 **One of your greatest strengths is:**

   a. your ability to keep calm in a crisis.

   b. your courage to speak up when you feel slighted.

   c. your fairness.

   d. your sense of style.

3 **Your school is having a dance and you're one of the organisers. It's your job to:**

   a. supervise the refreshments.

   b. hang up posters.

   c. take pictures at the event.

   d. decorate the hall.

4 **Which would you rather do?**

   a. Save someone's life

   b. Fight for what you believe in

   c. Tell a story that needs to be heard

   d. Make people look and feel good

5 If you could think of one word to describe you, it would be:

a. compassionate.

b. outspoken.

c. curious.

d. chic.

6 You'd never:

a. faint at the sight of blood.

b. give up without a fight.

c. ignore your inner voice.

d. leave the house without a last look in the mirror.

7 If you have to be assigned homework, you'd rather tackle:

a. a maths problem.

b. a history essay.

c. a classic novel.

d. an oral presentation.

8 If you could volunteer after school, you'd:

a. help out at your local hospital.

b. answer the phones at a law office.

c. be an intern at the local newspaper.

d. lend a hand at a charity ball or fundraiser.

ANSWERS

Mostly A's
Medically Minded

You'd make a great doctor or nurse because you're calm under pressure and aren't the least bit squeamish. Plus, maths and science actually make sense to you – and you're going to need them to get through medical school.

Mostly B's
Legal Eagle

Your ability to speak your mind would serve you well as a lawyer or judge. You've got a lot of important things to say. Where better to do that than in a courtroom?

Mostly C's
Nose for News

You're curious by nature and never quite believe what you hear – at least until you've done some investigating. You also like to write, which is a winning combination for a reporter or magazine editor.

Mostly D's
Fearless Fashionista

You always know what – and what not – to wear. Plus, you like helping your friends and family choose clothes. You're gifted at sketching too, which would make you a great clothing designer. Move over, Matthew Williamson!

How **WELL** Do You Know **YOUR BEST FRIEND**?

Make copies of this quiz to give to your friends — or read the sentences out loud.

Answer the questions below and then swap sheets to find out how much you really know about each other.

ALL ABOUT ME: (your name)

1 My middle name is:

2 My mother's occupation is:

3 My father's occupation is:

4 My favourite pizza topping is:

5 My favourite colour is:

6 My pets names are:

7 My favourite TV programme is:

8 My favourite band is:

9 I would rather die than:

10 My deepest secret is:

11 My worst fear is:

12 The one thing that really makes me mad is:

13 My biggest celebrity crush is:

14 I am secretly in love with:

ALL ABOUT HER: (your friend's name)

1 Her middle name is:

2 Her mother's occupation is:

3 Her father's occupation is:

4 Her favourite pizza topping is:

5 Her favourite colour is:

6 Her pets names are:

7 Her favourite TV programme is:

8 Her favourite band is:

9 She would rather die than:

10 Her deepest secret is:

11 Her worst fear is:

12 The one thing that really makes her mad is:

13 Her biggest celebrity crush is:

14 She is secretly in love with

ANSWERS   Give yourself one point for every correct answer. Your score:

11–14 points
SHARING THE SAME BRAIN
Are you sure you weren't Siamese twins separated at birth? You know each other inside and out. That goes to show that you're both great listeners and are totally in tune with one another.

6–10 points
GETTING TO KNOW YOU
You know your friend well but there's always something new to learn about her or to share about yourself, which is what keeps your friendship going strong. The more you hang out, the more you'll know!

0–5 points
HAVE WE MET?
Are you sure you two are best friends? Because you don't seem to know very much about one another! Try paying more attention when you are talking – you just might learn something you didn't know.

What Does Your Handwriting Reveal About You?

The way you write can decode some of the secrets of your psyche. Grab a pen and find out what yours is trying to tell you.

First, copy the following paragraph on unlined paper in joined-up writing:

I wonder what my handwriting reveals about my personality. Will it show that I am serious or silly? Calm or hyper? Maybe it will show that I love to have fun.

[Your signature]

HOW DOES YOUR HANDWRITING SLANT?

   a. To the right

   b. To the left

   c. Somewhere in between

A right slant is the most common and means that you are a warm, outgoing person. It can also show that you are impatient or wrote in a hurry. Writers who slant toward the left are generally more reserved. It is important for you to be true to yourself; you do not like being pressured by others. An in-between, or vertical slant, shows that you are disciplined and focused.

WHICH BEST DESCRIBES YOUR LETTERS?

   a. Tiny

   b. Large and easy to read

   c. Neither large nor small

Small letters are often a sign of modesty. You don't like to share your emotions. Large handwriting signals an outgoing person who loves to socialize. Medium-sized letters show a well-balanced person. You have the ability to think through situations and would be great in business.

THE INK IS:

   a. dark. You pressed down hard on the pen.

   b. light.

People who have dark penmanship often have a lot of inner strength. Pressing lightly on your pen may be a sign that you're unsure of yourself.

THE SPACE BETWEEN EACH LINE IS:

   a. wide.

   b. narrow.

If you leave a lot of space between lines you are an observant person. You like to watch what's going on around you before making decisions. If your writing is close together, you're a calm person. You don't lose your cool under pressure.

THE LETTERS IN EACH WORD ARE:

   a. connected.

   b. broken.

If you connect your letters fluidly, you are a perfectionist and have a positive attitude. Gaps between letters may mean you're a dreamer and are very expressive.

What's Your BEST QUALITY?

Everyone has something that makes her special. What is it that makes you great?

1 You overhear someone saying nasty things about you at school. You:

a. ask her if you've done something to offend her.

b. ignore her. Who cares what she thinks?

c. are terribly hurt – you try to be nice to everyone.

d. Confront her in front of the whole school. No one talks about you and gets away with it.

2 Your best friend is having a lot of problems with her mum. She comes to you because:

a. you'll be completely honest with her no matter what.

b. you can help her see that her problems aren't as bad as she thinks.

c. you are a great listener and don't judge her.

d. you always know how to make her feel better.

3 In family discussions, you:

a. can give your opinion without offending anyone.

b. can keep everyone from getting too excited.

c. get very emotional.

d. always speak your mind.

4 Your sister wants to try out for the tennis team, but she can't hit the ball to save her life. You:

a. gently tell her that a sport that doesn't require hand-eye coordination might be best for her.

b. tell her to go for it. If she doesn't make it, so what?

c. agree to help her practice her serve every day after school.

d. convince her to try out for the drama club with you instead. It's way cooler.

5 You expect your friends to:

a. always tell you the truth.

b. keep you from stressing out all the time.

c. keep your secrets.

d. know how to have fun.

6 You got a D on your maths test. When your parents ask you how you're going to improve your marks, you:

a. ask if they can get you a tutor. Those algebra equations are a killer!

b. tell them you've got it under control. If you don't get a better grade on your next quiz, you'll forgo watching TV for a month.

c. say that you plan to study every night for 30 minutes – even on weekends.

d. explain that you've got more important things to worry about. How often do they use algebra in their daily lives anyway?

7 You're out shopping with a friend when she shoplifts a pair of earrings. You:

a. make her go back to the store and admit what she did. It's wrong and she knows it.

b. pretend not to notice. If she gets caught, you aren't going down with her.

c. tell the store manager the next time you're in there that they really should get some security cameras.

d. marvel at her nerve and compliment her taste, but tell her to be careful!

8 You'd like to think you are:

a. trustworthy.

b. laidback.

c. loyal and nice.

d. clever and funny.

ANSWERS

Mostly A's
HONEST AND TRUE

You put a high priority on the truth and your friends trust that you'll tell them what you really think. Always sincere, you don't like people who lie or cheat and you try not to associate with them.

Mostly B's
CALM AND CAREFREE

You don't let anything get to you. You're a happy, free spirit and you try to enjoy life. You already know that if you stressed out about every little problem, you'd never get anything done. Instead, you relax and go with the flow.

Mostly C's
THOROUGHLY THOUGHTFUL

You're as kind as they come and would never dream of hurting anyone. A loyal and dedicated friend, you always treat people with warmth and respect. You do not have any time for mean-spirited folks.

Mostly D's
FEISTY AND FUN

You love to have a good time and always speak your mind. There's never a dull moment when you're around. Because of your energy and contagious laughter, people love to hang out with you.

Are You Destined For STARDOM?

Do you seek the spotlight or is being behind the scenes more your bag?

START

You have to give an oral presentation for English class. You:

ask your teacher if you could possibly complete a written assignment instead.

practice your speech over and over every night before bed.

don't worry about it. You actually like public speaking.

It's Saturday afternoon and your friends want to hang out. They:

wait for you to call them with a game plan. You're the planner of the group.

let you know where to meet. You're up for anything.

the upcoming projects interest you.

Before you go out, you always:

you like the other members and can be on the planning committee.

You'll only join a club if:

you can be the president.

It's time to elect a captain for your football team. You:

start planning the best way to get your teammates to vote for you.

casually let it slip that your friend Sarah would make a great leader.

Your mum gets the photos back from your family vacation. You're:

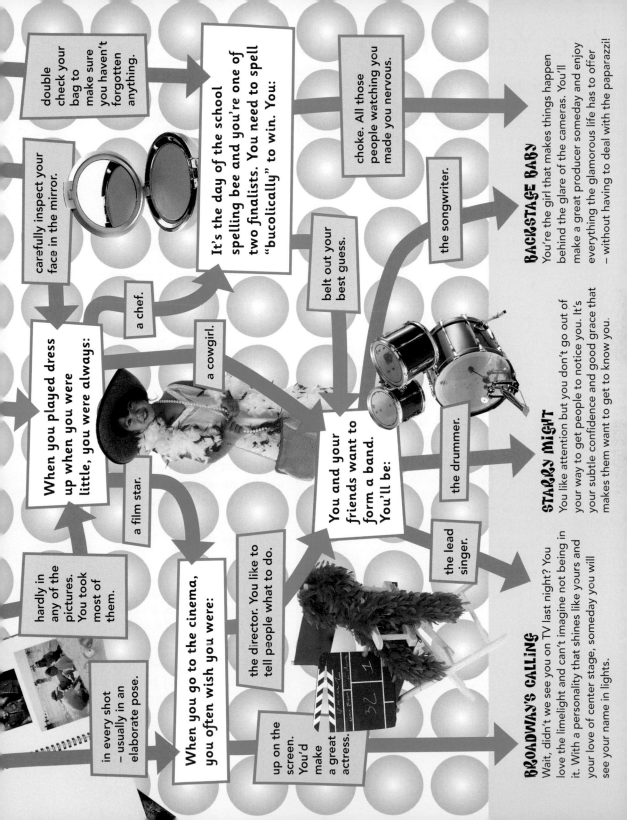

double check your bag to make sure you haven't forgotten anything.

carefully inspect your face in the mirror.

It's the day of the school spelling bee and you're one of two finalists. You need to spell "bucolically" to win. You:

choke. All those people watching you made you nervous.

a chef.

belt out your best guess.

the songwriter.

When you played dress up when you were little, you were always:

a cowgirl.

a film star.

You and your friends want to form a band. You'll be:

the drummer.

hardly in any of the pictures. You took most of them.

the director. You like to tell people what to do.

the lead singer.

in every shot – usually in an elaborate pose.

When you go to the cinema, you often wish you were:

up on the screen. You'd make a great actress.

BACKSTAGE BABY
You're the girl that makes things happen behind the glare of the cameras. You'll make a great producer someday and enjoy everything the glamorous life has to offer – without having to deal with the paparazzi!

STARRY MIGHT
You like attention but you don't go out of your way to get people to notice you. It's your subtle confidence and good grace that makes them want to get to know you.

BROADWAY'S CALLING
Wait, didn't we see you on TV last night? You love the limelight and can't imagine not being in it. With a personality that shines like yours and your love of center stage, someday you will see your name in lights.

Are You A Mean Girl?

You can't be sweet all of the time. But are you becoming more nasty than nice?

1 There's a boy in your science class who smells like he's been wearing the same socks for three weeks. You:

a. tip off your friends to hold their breath when you pass by him.

b. loudly ask if he's ever heard of soap and water.

c. feel really sorry for him and wonder if he has a medical condition that makes him smell so bad.

2 You think a friend might be talking about you behind your back. To find out for sure, you:

a. make another friend call her and start bad-mouthing you while you're secretly on the line.

b. come right out and ask her if she has a problem with you.

c. poll your friends for more information and advice.

3 Your really pretty friend just dyed her hair and it looks awful. When she asks you what you think, you:

a. say that its hard to top her natural look, since she's so beautiful.

b. laugh and say she needs to dye it back immediately.

c. lie and tell her it looks fabulous. Maybe now every guy in school will stop drooling over her.

4 The new girl in school wears really baggy, unstylish clothes. The next time you see her, you:

a. ask her how she'd describe her look. Homeless chic, perhaps?

b. invite her to come to the mall with you and your friends this weekend.

c. walk on by. She's clearly not interested in the same things as you.

5 Your best friend hates the band you're obsessed with. The next time she makes a remark, you:

a. tell her that her taste in tunes stinks.

b. agree to disagree.

c. force her to listen to their hit song and see if she still has the guts to say it's not the best song in the world.

6 A classmate who isn't in your circle of friends tries to sit at your lunch table. You:

a. let her.

b. give her an annoyed look but don't say anything.

c. say, "Excuse me, but I only eat lunch with people I like."

7 When you were little, a boy stole the toy you were playing with in the sand pit. You:

a. hid all of his toys where he would never find them.

b. cried.

c. demanded he give it back.

8 You and a friend like the same guy. To keep him from being interested in her, you:

a. tell him she's been seeing a doctor for an extreme case of bad breath.

b. flirt with him every chance you get.

c. make a habit of showing up every time she tries to talk to him.

9 You're on the hockey field and you and another teammate are both running for the ball. She's taking the lead. You:

a. push yourself to move faster.

b. trip her with your stick when the coach isn't looking.

c. try to cut her off at the pass.

10 You try out for the lead in the ballet and lose out to another dancer. On opening night, you:

a. secretly hope she twists her ankle so you can go on in her place.

b. go backstage to wish her luck and "accidentally" spill your drink all over her costume.

c. are in the audience cheering her on.

ANSWERS

1	a=2	b=3	c=1
2	a=3	b=2	c=1
3	a=1	b=2	c=3
4	a=3	b=1	c=2
5	a=3	b=1	c=2
6	a=1	b=2	c=3
7	a=3	b=1	c=2
8	a=3	b=1	c=2
9	a=1	b=3	c=2
10	a=2	b=3	c=1

24–30 Points
Little Green Meanie

Yikes! No one wants to be on your bad side. Sometimes you allow your temper or your insecurities to get the best of you. Remember: making others feel small doesn't make you feel big. When you sense a nasty comment coming on, take a deep breath and wait until your anger dies down.

17–23 points
Snide Streak

You may not always say rude things or consciously try to be mean, but sometimes your facial expressions or actions can be just as hurtful. Keep that in mind the next time you're tempted to roll your eyes or ignore someone. It takes fewer muscles to smile than to frown!

10–16 points
Perfectly Pleasant

You don't have a nasty bone in your body. In fact, you go out of your way to make others feel welcome and at ease, which goes to show that you are very comfortable with who you are. You are genuinely kind and caring and will never be at a loss for friends.

What Do Your Dreams Mean?

Whether you remember it or not, you dream every night of your life. And those mini-movies often are your subconscious's way of communicating with you. What are your dreams trying to say?

For a week, keep a diary beside your bed. As soon as you wake up, write down everything you remember about your dreams, including how they made you feel. Were you scared? Happy? Anxious? Peaceful? The following questions will help you decipher your dreams.

Did you dream in colour? If so, which one was strongest?

a. Red

b. Orange

c. Yellow

d. Green

e. Blue

f. White

g. Black

a Red could indicate anger or passion. If something is really bothering you, stay calm till you get all the facts straight.

b Orange is a bright colour for outgoing people. You are adventurous and certainly not afraid of new things.

c Yellow is the colour of hope and optimism. You are a positive person who sure knows how to look on the bright side of life!

d Green is the colour of progress and healing. You're a confident person who keeps growing and learning about yourself!

e Blue shows that you're good at expressing yourself. It is a calm and tranquil colour. Trust your deepest instincts.

f White may be the main colour of your dreams if you are about to embark on a new situation or say goodbye to a bad one. Enjoy!

g Black symbolises the unknown, which can be frightening. Learn to trust yourself, and your dreams will become more comforting.

Were any of the following situations in your dreams?

a. My teeth are falling out!

b. I am hanging out with celebrities.

c. I can't remember my lines.

d. I am in deep water.

e. There are spiders everywhere.

f. Oh no! I am naked! In public!

g. I never remember my dreams.

a You are feeling powerless or embarrassed. Brush up on your communication skills and make your voice heard!

b Chilling with the famous and fabulous may indicate that you have reached or about to reach one of your goals. Congratulations!

c Sounds like you're overbooked. Stress is making you frazzled. Take a bath, a nap or a long break, and you'll sleep better.

d Calm and clear water means you are happy and at ease with your life. Rough waves can mean you are feeling overwhelmed.

e Spiders may creep you out in real life, but they are good luck in your dreams. Expect exciting news!

f Is a big test coming up? Are you nervous about something? Your dreams indicate you're feeling vulnerable or anxious.

g Try to get a solid eight hours. If you can, switch off your alarm and wake up naturally. Also, try concentrating on a goal or question before bedtime.

What kind of animals appeared in your dreams?

a. Dogs
b. Dolphins
c. Cats
d. Bees
e. Lions
f. Bears
g. Sharks

a Protective and dependable, dogs are good omens. You must be surrounded by loving friends. But if it is a mean or angry dog, you may be questioning a friend's loyalty.

b Carefree yet trustworthy, dolphins often appear to soothe us or guide us through rough times. You have the support of your friends and things will get better soon.

c Uh-oh. Cats can mean you are in for some bad news. Be careful sharing your secrets. Don't worry if you are a big feline fan—cat lovers often dream of their favorite pets.

d Bees know how to work together in harmony and you may need that exact quality for a group project or sports team. Working together can be tough but keep up the hard work. It will pay off!

e Lions can show how you feel about yourself. You may be the social leader of your group or proud of yourself for doing something that required a great deal of courage.

f Have you been in a bad mood lately? Well, you're ready to move on. Or you may be competing with a rival. Like a bear, you're only aggressive when provoked.

g Sharks can symbolise your anger. Try to talk it out and you are sure to overcome the obstacles that seem to stand in your way.

Are you moving around in your dream?

a. Yes, I am flying.
b. Yes, but I feel like I am falling
c. Yes, I am running forward.
d. Yes, but I am being chased!
e. No, I am trying to run, but I can't. I'm stuck!
f. Yes, I am driving a car.
g. Yes, I am in a car, but I can't see where I am going!

a Flying may mean that you're trying to make changes in your life or that you are feeling so positive you are totally above the little problems in the world!

b Falling often occurs when you don't feel in control. If your parents are divorcing or you're fighting with a friend, your dreams can reflect your anxiety.

c Moving forward usually occurs in pleasant dreams that indicate things are going well for you right now. You probably feel safe and secure.

d Being chased can mean you're avoiding a problem. If you feel guilty about something or anxious about a confrontation, get it over with. You will sleep better!

e Being unable to run is frustrating when you are trying to get closer to something and terrifying when you are trying to get further away. You need a self-confidence boost!

f When you dream that you are driving, you are used to taking control of your waking life. You know yourself well and are comfortable making decisions.

g You might be unsure of a recent decision. If you are in the backseat, it could show that you depend on others a lot and shy away from taking charge.

How Much FUN Are You?

Are you always up for a good time or is party pooper your middle name?

1 You have a week off from school. You spend it:

   a. learning a new craft like knitting or jewellery-making.

   b. sleeping late and watching films.

   c. getting a head start on your homework.

2 You think you're going over to your cousin's house to hang out but when you get there, he surprises you with tickets to a concert. You're wearing jogging bottoms and a t-shirt. You:

   a. put on your coat and go to the show.

   b. agree to go only if he'll drive you home to change. Better late than not at all!

   c. say you can't go. Concerts are so loud and crowded anyway.

3 It's your birthday. You:

   a. throw a huge party for your entire class.

   b. have a couple of friends over for a sleepover.

   c. don't want to make a big deal of it.

4 In your family you're known as:

   a. "The giggler" because you love to laugh.

   b. "The planner" because you're very organised.

   c. "The quiet one" because you keep to yourself.

5 On long bus rides during school trips, you:

   a. tell everyone jokes.

   b. break out a deck of cards.

   c. curl up and take a nap.

6 A boy in your class dares you to throw a spitball at your maths teacher when he turns around. You:

   a. throw it.

   b. roll your eyes. Can you say immature?

   c. tell on him.

7 Your favourite song comes on the radio as you're getting ready for school. You:

a. dance around your room in your underwear.

b. turn it up so you can hear it over the hairdryer. You're running late.

c. quietly sing along. It is too early in the morning for jumping around.

8 You get invited to a party where you don't know any of the other guests. As soon as you arrive, you:

a. volunteer to handle the music. It isn't a party without good tunes.

b. start talking to the boy sitting next to you. Isn't he in your class?

c. head for the food table. That's always a safe bet.

9 You're really tired, but then your best friend calls and begs you to go shopping. You:

a. are instantly rejuvenated. You can't say no to a sale.

b. promise you'll go with her tomorrow if she can wait until then.

c. tell her you're not in the mood.

10 Your brother wants you to go bungee jumping with him. You:

a. say, "Name the time and the place."

b. tell him only if you can do it in tandem. You're afraid to jump alone.

c. ask him if he's lost his mind.

ANSWERS

Mostly A's
LIVELY LADY

You really know how to enjoy life! You're daring, adventurous and certainly never dull. People can always count on you to bring laughter and good times to any situation. Whether you are being the life of the party or babysitting the neighbour's kids, your personality sparkles.

Mostly B's
CAUTIOUSLY CAREFREE

Fun is definitely on your agenda but you are often the voice of reason among your friends. Yes, you'll go bungee jumping, but not before thoroughly researching the sport. You're practical and prepared but don't let it get in the way of a good time.

Mostly C's
NEED TO LOOSEN UP

You may be a bit uptight or overly shy and because of this, you could be missing out on some really exciting experiences. While you shouldn't do anything dangerous, the next time someone asks you to be spontaneous, go for it. You'll probably have a great time!

Can You Keep A SECRET?

Will you take it to the grave or does the urge to blab get the better of you?

1 A friend tells you something really personal about herself and asks you not to tell anyone else. How many people have you told?

a. None. You're a woman of your word.

b. One. You had to tell somebody!

c. Two. Okay, maybe four or five. You just couldn't help yourself.

2 Your mum's planning a surprise sweet sixteen party for your sister and tonight's the big night. When your sis starts fishing for clues, you:

a. tell her you don't know what she's doing this evening, but you're having a few girlfriends over to hang out. That'll confuse her!

b. blurt out every detail – including the video montage that your mum spent weeks putting together.

c. feign ignorance and then quickly leave the room. You don't want to crack under the pressure.

3 You find out that a friend's dad just lost his job. She doesn't want anyone to know. When your other friends ask you why she's been so sad, you:

a. tell them the real reason but ask them not to say anything to her.

b. say you have no idea and leave it at that.

c. make up something about her cat being really sick.

4 You're in the football coach's office and accidentally see the new team sheet. You are captain! You:

a. let your close friends know but that's it. How exciting!

b. wait for the coach to announce it to the team. You don't want her to think you were snooping.

c. start spreading the news. This is the best thing that's ever happened to you! You can't help it!

5 You overhear a really juicy piece of gossip but you're not sure if it's true. What do you with the information?

a. Forget about it. You don't like to spread rumours.

b. Tell your closest friends. If it is true, it's such a scandal!

c. File it away in the back of your mind until you get more details.

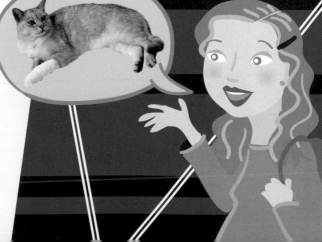

6 You open the hall cupboard and spot your brother's Christmas presents hidden behind some old coats. You:

a. quickly look away.

b. shuffle through them and then immediately let him know what to expect under the tree.

c. taunt him by saying "I know what you're getting," until he threatens you with bodily harm if you don't tell.

7 You overhear your aunt telling your mom that she thinks she's pregnant. You:

a. start brainstorming baby names so you will be ready with suggestions when the news is official.

b. spill to your siblings. So what if she's not completely sure yet? This is too good to keep to yourself.

c. hint to your aunt that she's got a special glow, and wait for her to tell you the news.

8 You read your sister's journal and learn that she has a huge crush on a boy named James, who's a family friend. You:

a. threaten to tell unless she lets you raid her wardrobe whenever you want.

b. tell your mum. She's been trying to fix the two of them up forever!

c. feel guilty that you read her private thoughts and vow not to peek again.

9 You read the spoiler alert for your favourite TV show and now know what's going to happen on the season finale. You:

a. tell your friends not to bother watching anymore. The main character leaves her husband for the gardener.

b. wish you hadn't kept reading. Now the thrill is gone.

c. tell your friends that you know the details of the shocking finale but you won't divulge it unless they ask you to.

ANSWERS

1 a=3 b=2 c=1
2 a=3 b=1 c=2
3 a=1 b=3 c=2
4 a=2 b=3 c=1
5 a=3 b=1 c=2
6 a=3 b=1 c=2
7 a=3 b=1 c=2
8 a=2 b=1 c=3
9 a=1 b=3 c=2

9–15 points
JABBER JAWS

Telling you a secret is like putting it in the newspaper. You have a really big mouth and the momentary satisfaction you get from gossiping tends to become more important than the pain your friends will feel when they find out you betrayed them. The next time you're tempted, try putting yourself in their shoes. You'll see that it's not a good place to be.

16–21 points
WILL TO SPILL

You're usually pretty good about keeping confidences, but you have spilled a secret before. It's hard to keep quiet, but you don't want to hurt anyone's feelings. Next time you get the urge to talk, type what you know on your computer and then delete it. That'll help you get the release you need, without causing anyone harm.

22–27 Points
LIPS ARE SEALED

Always a trustworthy friend, you believe in treating people – especially your friends – with respect, and that means you are fantastic at keeping secrets. When a friend asks you not to repeat something they've told you, you take it as a solemn promise. And you expect the same in return. The quickest way to get on your bad side is to break your trust.

Do You Hold A Grudge?

Can you forgive and forget or is forgiveness hard enough?
Follow the arrows and find out.

START

Have you stopped being friends with someone after a fight, even if it was over something silly?

No

Yes

Yes, but eventually you both apologised and are friendly again

You've got a starring role in the school play and your older sister is missing opening night to go on spring break with her girlfriends. You:

wish she could be there, but know that fun in the sun is hard to pass up.

are secretly seething. How could she miss your dramatic debut?

If you found out someone lied to you:

you would make sure to double check the facts. Maybe it was a misunderstanding?

you'd probably be angry, but it would depend on how big the lie was.

you'd be deeply hurt. Lying is the worst thing someone could do to you.

You help your friend study for a test and she gets a higher mark than you do! You:

You find out that a casual acquaintance kissed the boy you like. You:

vow never to speak to her again. Oh, the betrayal!

are upset, but tell yourself that if he likes her instead of you, it's his loss.

You and Marisa are best friends now, but you hated each other when you were little. So it's not surprising that you were the only girl in the class who didn't get invited to her 7th birthday party. Six years later, you:

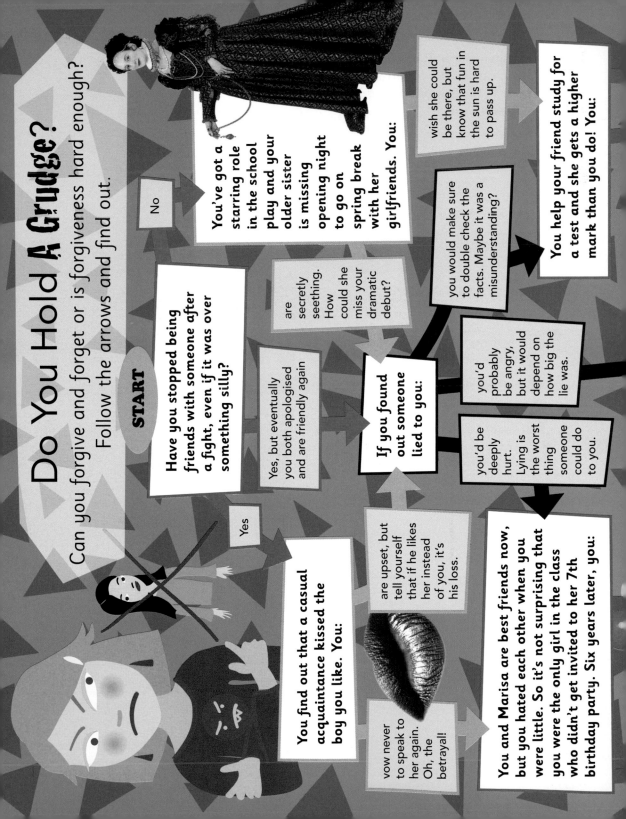

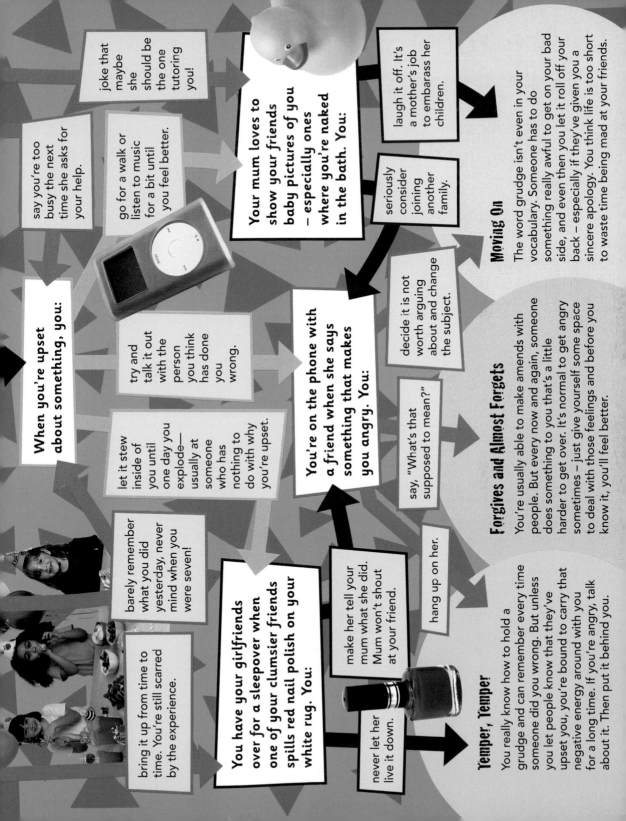

When you're upset about something, you:

say you're too busy the next time she asks for your help.

go for a walk or listen to music for a bit until you feel better.

try and talk it out with the person you think has done you wrong.

let it stew inside of you until one day you explode—usually at someone who has nothing to do with why you're upset.

joke that maybe she should be the one tutoring you!

Your mum loves to show your friends baby pictures of you – especially ones where you're naked in the bath. You:

laugh it off. It's a mother's job to embarass her children.

seriously consider joining another family.

You're on the phone with a friend when she says something that makes you angry. You:

decide it is not worth arguing about and change the subject.

say, "What's that supposed to mean?"

hang up on her.

barely remember what you did yesterday, never mind when you were seven!

bring it up from time to time. You're still scarred by the experience.

You have your girlfriends over for a sleepover when one of your clumsier friends spills red nail polish on your white rug. You:

make her tell your mum what she did. Mum won't shout at your friend.

never let her live it down.

Moving On

The word grudge isn't even in your vocabulary. Someone has to do something really awful to get on your bad side, and even then you let it roll off your back – especially if they've given you a sincere apology. You think life is too short to waste time being mad at your friends.

Forgives and Almost Forgets

You're usually able to make amends with people. But every now and again, someone does something to you that's a little harder to get over. It's normal to get angry sometimes – just give yourself some space to deal with those feelings and before you know it, you'll feel better.

Temper, Temper!

You really know how to hold a grudge and can remember every time someone did you wrong. But unless you let people know that they've upset you, you're bound to carry that negative energy around with you for a long time. If you're angry, talk about it. Then put it behind you.

Are You Too STRESSED OUT?

Is your schedule making you crazy?

1 **Your history teacher gives your class a huge project – and it's due at the end of the week. You:**

a. hit the library after school. If you work on it for an hour each day, you should be fine.

b. are worried, but know that you'll get it done. You always do.

c. panic. There is absolutely no way you'll ever finish.

2 **When you wake up in the morning, you often feel:**

a. refreshed and ready to start your day.

b. sometimes refreshed, other times tired. It depends on when you went to bed.

c. exhausted. You have nightmares and toss and turn all night.

3 **Your best friend wants you to hang out, your mum needs your help cooking dinner, and you've got to practise your saxophone if you hope to make the band. You:**

a. decide that watching TV is about all you can handle and spend the rest of the afternoon on the sofa.

b. tell your best friend that you'll see her later, make a deal with your mum that if she cooks, you'll do the dishes and then get to work on your music.

c. flop on the bed and start to cry. It is impossible to do it all!

4 **You often feel like:**

a. you're not busy enough.

b. you have a lot going on, but you can handle it.

c. you're totally overwhelmed.

5 **Auditions for the school play are tomorrow. You:**

a. go to bed at a decent hour, so you're fully rested for the big day.

b. get up early to for a morning paractice session.

c. practice smiling and breathing so you don't pass out.

6 **You have to give an oral presentation in class. You:**

a. wing it. You've never had a problem speaking in public.

b. say your speech ten times in front of your mirror.

c. think you might throw up before it's your turn.

7 **In your free time, you like to:**

a. relax.

b. hang out with friends and catch up on your reading.

c. . . . free time? Who has free time?!

8 **You've got a maths test tomorrow and you haven't started studying yet. You:**

a. don't sweat it. You know this stuff inside out.

b. start hitting the books as soon as you finish dinner.

c. consider pretending to be sick. There's no way you're going to pass.

9 **At least once a day you feel like:**

a. taking a break.

b. you're forgetting something.

c. screaming.

10 **When you get ready to leave for school in the morning, you:**

a. double check your outfit in the mirror.

b. check to see that you have your homework.

c. make sure you have packed your school books, your homework, your lunch, a snack for before practice and a bag for each of your afterschool activities.

ANSWERS

Mostly A's
CALM AS THEY COME

Nothing rattles you. You keep your cool in the most stressful situations. But sometimes being so laid back can come off as laziness. As long as you don't start slacking off, you can just relax and enjoy.

Mostly B's
SLIGHTLY STRESSED

You're a busy girl and sometimes all that pressure gets to you. Luckily, you know how to stay organised and take good care of yourself. A positive attitude is a huge plus for a busy person like you.

Mostly C's
ANXIETY ATTACK

You are one step away from a panic attack! You're letting your nerves take over your life. Try cutting back on your activities or taking an afternoon off. You will feel better, sleep better and have more fun. Take a break: you deserve it!

How Well Do You Listen?

Pardon? What'd you say? Find out if you're in tune with what's happening around you.

1 Your teacher asks you a question in class. You:

a. answer with confidence.

b. rack your brain to come up with the correct answer. Was this part of your homework?

c. have no idea what she's talking about. You were too busy passing notes with your best friend.

2 You're on the phone with a girlfriend who's going through a major crisis. What else are you doing?

a. Sitting in your favourite chair, totally engrossed

b. Half-watching TV

c. Instant Messenging with a guy in your class

3 Your friend tells you she can't hang out after school. You:

a. say OK and tell her you'll call her later.

b. think she probably just needs time by herself.

c. take it as sign that your friendship is over.

4 Your mum asks you to stop at the shop on your way home from school and pick up milk and a dozen eggs. You:

a. come home with milk and a dozen eggs.

b. get some mint chocolate chip ice cream while you're at it. She didn't say to *only* buy milk and eggs.

c. have to call her on your mobile phone from the shop. Did she say milk or orange juice?

5 In French class, you often have to listen to audio tapes and then write down what the speakers are saying. You:

a. breeze through it.

b. concentrate really hard. Are they talking about biking or hiking?

c. hate this exercise. You can never keep up with them.

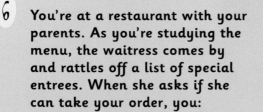

8 It's your best friend's birthday and she's been hinting about a really cute pair of earrings she saw. You:

a. track down the earrings that she won't stop talking about.

b. buy her earrings that look like the ones she wanted. They both have red stones. Or was it pink?

c. get her a funky scarf. It's so her.

9 Two of your friends are talking to you at once. You:

a. give each of them an ear. You're good at multi-tasking.

b. tell them you can only focus on one person at a time.

c. wait until they are both finished and say, "What?"

6 You're at a restaurant with your parents. As you're studying the menu, the waitress comes by and rattles off a list of special entrees. When she asks if she can take your order, you:

a. tell her you need a few more minutes to decide. Everything sounds yummy!

b. ask her if she can repeat the pasta special.

c. ask her what the specials are.

7 You're going to a new friend's house. She's just given you directions. When you get in the car with your dad, you:

a. are all set. You took careful notes.

b. think you remember what she said.

c. are thankful that your dad's car has satellite navigation. You have no idea where you're going.

answers

Mostly A's
Really Good Ear

When a friend needs to talk, they know you're the one to go to. You're focused, make eye contact and genuinely seem to care about what they have to say. From recalling directions to remembering friends' likes and dislikes, being a good listener will serve you well throughout life.

Mostly B's
Awesome Effort

You try hard to pay attention to people, but sometimes you can't help letting your mind wander. You're a busy girl so it's not surprising you want to veg out sometimes. If you're tired or are having trouble concentrating, say so. It's better than ignoring someone.

Mostly C's
One More Time?

You get distracted easily, probably because you're always trying to do several things at once. So, you are not really concentrating on any one thing. Make an effort to give people your full attention; it will save you from misunderstandings in the future.

Do You **STAND UP** For Yourself?

Are you a doormat or do you know how to take charge?

START

You had plans to hang out with a friend after school and she cancelled — again. You:

- jump at the chance to meet up the next time she calls. She's so much fun.
- let her know that your time is valuable too and that you expect a phone call if plans change.
- call her and shout that if she ditches you again, the friendship is over.

One of your classmates constantly teases you in front of the other kids. You:

- grin and bear it. You don't want to make things worse by responding.
- tell him that 1999 called. It wants its hairstyle back.

You're playing cards with your friends when you notice one of them is cheating. You:

- go to her house. It's much easier to go than to listen to her throw a fit.
- tell her that she's not the boss of you and you don't feel like hanging out today.

One of the girls in your group is really bossy. Today, she told all of you that if you don't come to her house after school, you're no longer her friends. You:

- gather your friends together to confront her. This is the last straw—her bossy days are over!

Your cousin tells one of his teammates that he "throws like a girl." You:

- agree that his friend's arm could use some work.
- shoot back that your cousin only wishes he could lob a ball as hard as you can.

Your brother breaks your mum's really expensive antique vase. He tells her you did it. You:

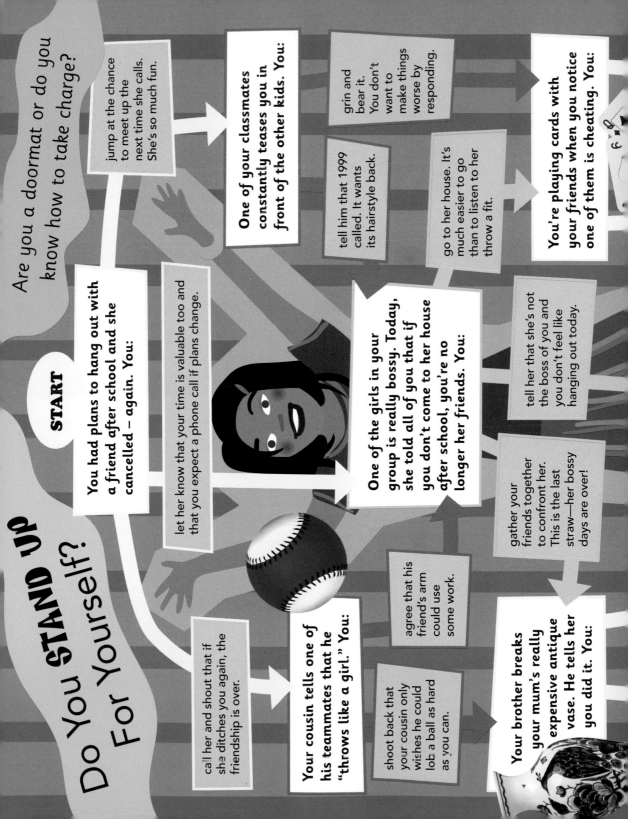

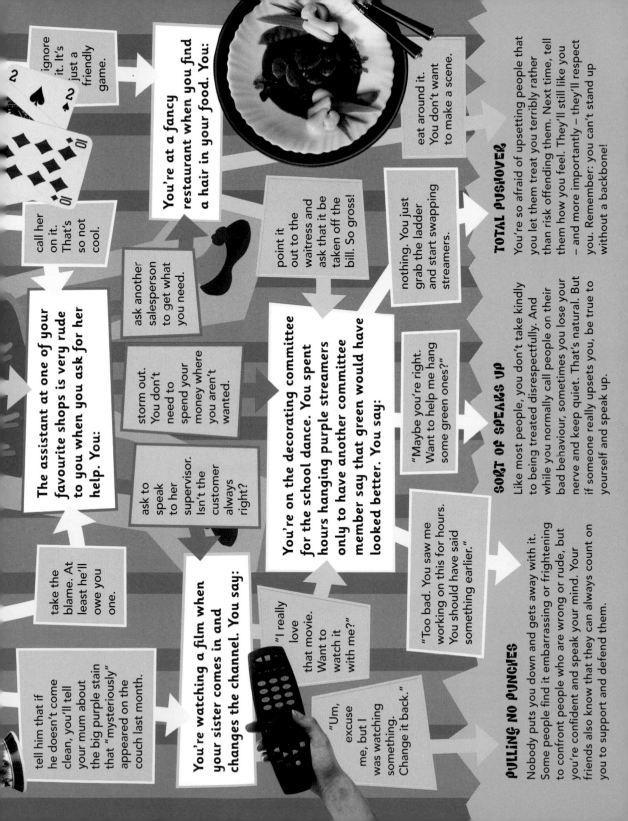

ignore it. It's just a friendly game.

You're at a fancy restaurant when you find a hair in your food. You:

eat around it. You don't want to make a scene.

call her on it. That's so not cool.

ask another salesperson to get what you need.

point it out to the waitress and ask that it be taken off the bill. So gross!

nothing. You just grab the ladder and start swapping streamers.

TOTAL PUSHOVER

You're so afraid of upsetting people that you let them treat you terribly rather than risk offending them. Next time, tell them how you feel. They'll still like you – and more importantly – they'll respect you. Remember: you can't stand up without a backbone!

The assistant at one of your favourite shops is very rude to you when you ask for her help. You:

storm out. You don't need to spend your money where you aren't wanted.

ask to speak to her supervisor. Isn't the customer always right?

You're on the decorating committee for the school dance. You spent hours hanging purple streamers only to have another committee member say that green would have looked better. You say:

"Maybe you're right. Want to help me hang some green ones?"

SORT OF SPEAKS UP

Like most people, you don't take kindly to being treated disrespectfully. And while you normally call people on their bad behaviour, sometimes you lose your nerve and keep quiet. That's natural. But if someone really upsets you, be true to yourself and speak up.

take the blame. At least he'll owe you one.

tell him that if he doesn't come clean, you'll tell your mum about the big purple stain that "mysteriously" appeared on the couch last month.

You're watching a film when your sister comes in and changes the channel. You say:

"I really love that movie. Want to watch it with me?"

"Too bad. You saw me working on this for hours. You should have said something earlier."

"Um, excuse me, but I was watching something. Change it back."

PULLING NO PUNCHES

Nobody puts you down and gets away with it. Some people find it embarrassing or frightening to confront people who are wrong or rude, but you're confident and speak your mind. Your friends also know that they can always count on you to support and defend them.

Are You Ready For A Boyfriend?

Thinking about becoming a twosome? Take this quiz to see if the time is now.

1 The thought of kissing a boy is:

a. really appealing.

b. interesting, but a little scary.

c. kind of gross.

2 You catch one of the guys in your class staring at you during the teacher's super boring lecture. You:

a. look away.

b. hold his gaze for a few seconds and then turn your attention back to your notebook.

c. flash him a wide smile.

3 A cutie asks you if you want to go to the cinema on Friday night. You say:

a. "I'd love to, but I promised my friend I'd hang out with her. Do you have any cute friends who can come along?"

b. "What time?"

c. "Sounds cool. Who else is going?"

4 You catch your sister and her boyfriend kissing. You:

a. can't imagine yourself ever feeling comfortable enough to do that.

b. make a point to ask her later about her first kiss.

c. can't wait for that to be you.

5 You just got home from school and the phone rings. Your mum answers and tells you it's a boy – the one you have a little crush on. What do you do?

a. Take a deep breath and say hi, all the while praying you don't say anything stupid

b. Tell her you can't talk and then run and hide in your room

c. Pick up and just say hello

6 You're waiting for a ride home from school when a super cute football player strikes up a conversation with you. You:

   a. tell him you're thinking of going out for the girls' team. Maybe he can give you pointers some time.

   b. congratulate him on his amazing performance at yesterday's game.

   c. hope he stops talking soon. You really have nothing to say.

7 You like a guy. And you think he likes you. You've talked a little bit in school and now you're in the hall watching a school concert. Slowly, he puts his arm around your chair. You:

   a. freeze for a second and then relax. This is kind of nice.

   b. slowly inch your way a little closer to him. He smells really nice.

   c. get up and go to the bathroom.

8 In your circle of friends, how many of you have boyfriends?

   a. None

   b. About half

   c. All of them

9 You go for a run in your neighbourhood. As you're rounding the corner, you bump into a kid you've known since childhood, but haven't seen in awhile. He's really grown up! When he asks if you need a running partner, you say:

   a. "Yes, if you think you can keep up with me."

   b. "Actually I really like running alone. It clears my head."

   c. "I'd love one."

10 A guy you like asks you if you'll be his girlfriend. You:

   a. completely freeze up.

   b. say yes immediately.

   c. smile shyly and nod.

ANSWERS

1 a=3 b=2 c=1
2 a=1 b=2 c=3
3 a=2 b=3 c=1
4 a=1 b=2 c=3
5 a=2 b=1 c=3
6 a=3 b=2 c=1
7 a=2 b=3 c=1
8 a=1 b=2 c=3
9 a=3 b=1 c=2
10 a=1 b=3 c=2

24–30 Points
Yes, You Are!

Flirting comes naturally to you, and you feel at ease around guys. Plus, you've outgrown the "boys are icky stage" which is key. Just don't rush into anything. Your confidence is extra-attractive, so keep smiling and meeting people. When the right boy appears on the scene, you'll know.

17–23 points
Getting Warmer

So, you aren't a flirting whiz just yet. That's no big deal. You may get a bit shy, tongue-tied or goofy when a member of the opposite sex talks to you, but that could be because you aren't used to it. Try talking to boys in your class or other group activities and you'll get better at it!

10–16 Points
So Not Ready

Boys scare you. But it's a good bet you're not the only one. (In fact, a lot of guys are probably terrified of us girls!) You've got plenty of time for relationships later, so don't feel like you need to do anything that you aren't ready for. When the time is right, it'll all become clear.

Are You Too Competitive?

Will you do anything to win or is the joy of the game enough?

1 You're playing badminton at a family picnic. It's you and your brother against your cousins. You:

a. practically knock your brother out as you attempt a killer serve. The other team is going down!

b. had forgotten how much fun this game really is.

c. make a friendly bet with your cousins about who's the best player.

2 You've just recently taken up chess. To get better at it, you:

a. start playing more.

b. read every book about the game and bully your friends into playing with you twice a week. Maybe you could be a champion player some day.

c. challenge your brother to a match. Loser does the dishes for a week.

3 Your team loses the basketball championship because one of your teammates choked on her last shot. You:

a. give her a hug and tell her there's always next year. You know she tried her best.

b. are really upset but try not to show it. What's done is done.

c. can't help screaming at her as she comes off the court. That last throw she made was just ridiculous!

4 You and your best friend are in all the same classes. Every time you have a test, you:

a. try to study together. Two brains are better than one.

b. ask her what mark she got. You want to be top of the class.

c. mention your own mark, and wait for her to reveal hers. You are just curious.

5 Your sister is five years older than you are, but you're often compared to her. The next time someone says how much you remind him of her, you:

a. take it as a compliment, as usual. She's a great girl.

b. say you really don't see the similarities.

c. point out how superior you are to her in school, sports and even looks.

6 Your motto is:

a. "If you can't be the best at what you do, there's no point in doing it."

b. "Practice makes perfect."

c. "If you believe in yourself, anything is possible."

7 You come in third place at an equestrian competition. You:

a. are shocked. You didn't think you had a chance.

b. feel happy, but know you can do better next time.

c. throw your ribbon in the rubbish bin on the way out. Third is unacceptable.

8 Your friend bought a really cute printed bag. You:

a. buy a bigger, more expensive version.

b. wish you could pull off a wild look like that.

c. tell her how good it looks with her outfit.

9 You go on a bike ride with your friends. You:

a. challenge them to a race.

b. leisurely pedal along and enjoy the sunshine and scenery.

c. don't speak the whole time you're riding. You're in the zone and don't want to lose focus.

ANSWERS

1 a=3	b=1	c=2
2 a=1	b=3	c=2
3 a=1	b=3	c=3
4 a=1	b=3	c=2
5 a=1	b=2	c=3
6 a=3	b=2	c=1
7 a=1	b=2	c=3
8 a=3	b=2	c=1
9 a=2	b=1	c=3

9–15 Points
Team Player

For you, working together and having fun are key. If you spend more time laughing than winning while playing video games, you've had a great day. You want everyone you care about to succeed and you'll do whatever you can to make that happen. Your generosity of spirit is one of your greatest assets.

16–21 Points
Hate to Lose

You play to win, but if you don't get a bullseye every time, you try not to let it get to you. As long as you gave it your best shot, you can't be too hard on yourself. You like to have good-natured contests with friends but, in the end, your relationships are way more important than taking home the trophy.

22–27 Points
All About Winning

You've got a serious competitive streak. You let winning become the most important thing. Your pride in your abilities gives you a great boost on the field, in the pool or on the court. But if your urge to win comes at the expense of your friends' or family's feelings, that's a trade off not worth making.

How Healthy Are You?

You look good, but are you taking the best care of yourself?

1 **You come home from school and need a snack. You reach for:**

a. an orange.

b. fresh fruit and yoghurt.

c. chocolate chip cookies.

2 **You've decided to take up running. The first day, you:**

a. push yourself to do five miles.

b. decide to start with one mile and see how you feel.

c. make it once around the block before passing out from exhaustion.

3 **At night, you get _____ hours of sleep.**

a. 10 to 12

b. 7 or 8

c. less than 6

4 **When you go out in the sun, you wear sunscreen:**

a. sometimes.

b. always.

c. almost never.

5 **You get sick:**

a. occasionally.

b. rarely.

c. a lot.

6 **How many glasses of water do you drink a day?**

a. Three or four

b. Six to eight

c. One maybe – you prefer cola or juice

7 **How many hours of TV do you watch every day?**

a. One – you've picked one thing to watch when you are done with your homework

b. Two or three after school and on weekends

c. Four or more – and even more than that on weekends

ANSWERS

Mostly A's
Health on the Brain

You try to eat healthy and get just the right amount of sleep, but you don't always do both. Increase your water intake, and add a little more protein to your diet to really be at the top of your game. Find an exercise class or activity you love it will make healthy habits easier to maintain.

Mostly B's
Tip Top Shape

Congratulations! It sounds like you know what your body needs for solid health. As long as you keep exercising, staying hydrated, eating well-balanced meals, using sunscreen and taking multi-vitamins, you'll remain way above the curve. If only everyone followed your example!

Mostly C's
Needs Some Work

Instead of snacking on cola and cookies, try injecting a little fruit and veg into your diet. And please, wear sunscreen! Your skin will thank you for it when you're 40! With just a little more time spent walking, cycling, dancing or swimming and a little less time on the sofa, you'll feel much healthier!

Does He LIKE You?

He's caught your eye, but does he feel the same?

1 He sees you in the corridor at school. What does he do?

a. Says hello and smiles

b. Nods at you and keeps walking

c. Ignores you

2 You leave a Valentine in his locker – and are brave enough to sign your name. He:

a. doesn't say anything to you directly, but tells your best friend he thought it was romantic.

b. gives you a Valentine in return.

c. doesn't let on that he received it.

3 You're walking home from school alone as he rides his bike. He:

a. waves as he goes past.

b. shouts your name and smiles.

c. stops to talk.

4 He sits with you and your friends at lunch. He talks to:

a. you, mostly.

b. everyone.

c. your best friend. And come to think of it, he's sitting awfully close to her!

5 You forget your maths homework at home. He:

a. offers to let you copy his.

b. suggests that you tell the teacher what happened.

c. says, "That's a shame."

6 He has a party and asks you to come. When you arrive, he:

a. nods and goes back to his video game.

b. greets you at the door and introduces you to anyone you don't know.

c. makes his way over to you eventually and thanks you for coming.

ANSWERS

1 a=3 b=2 c=1

2 a=2 b=3 c=1

3 a=1 b=2 c=3

4 a=3 b=2 c=1

5 a=3 b=2 c=1

6 a=1 b=3 c=2

6–9 Points
DOES HE LIKE ANYONE?
If he's not giving you attention now, it doesn't mean he never will. Maybe he's shy or just not yet ready to flirt with you. Try talking to him more and see if he opens up.

10–13 Points
COULD GO EITHER WAY
Boys are tricky. You can't always tell what they're thinking. He knows you're alive and he just might be interested. Give it a little time and see what develops.

14–18 points
SURE BET
Unless this guy is your closest friend from childhood, it sounds like he is totally into you. He is giving you all the signs, so if you like him too, let him know!

Do You TALK Too Much?

Are you a motor mouth or a woman of few words? Follow the arrows to find out.

START

Your teacher calls for complete silence in class. You:

zip your lips.

switch to a whisper. You're in the middle of an important conversation!

After a phone conversation with a friend, you often feel:

like she did all of the talking.

thirsty!

Oral presentations are:

your worst nightmare.

your favourite type of homework assignment.

You're watching a foreign film that has subtitles. You read them:

in your head.

aloud.

You've been known to strike up conversations with people you meet on the bus or in queues for the ladies toilet!

You get into an argument with your parents. Who has the last word?

Them

You

At the dinner table, when your parents ask you how your day was, you:

mumble something about it being fine.

can go on for hours. They'll never believe what happened!

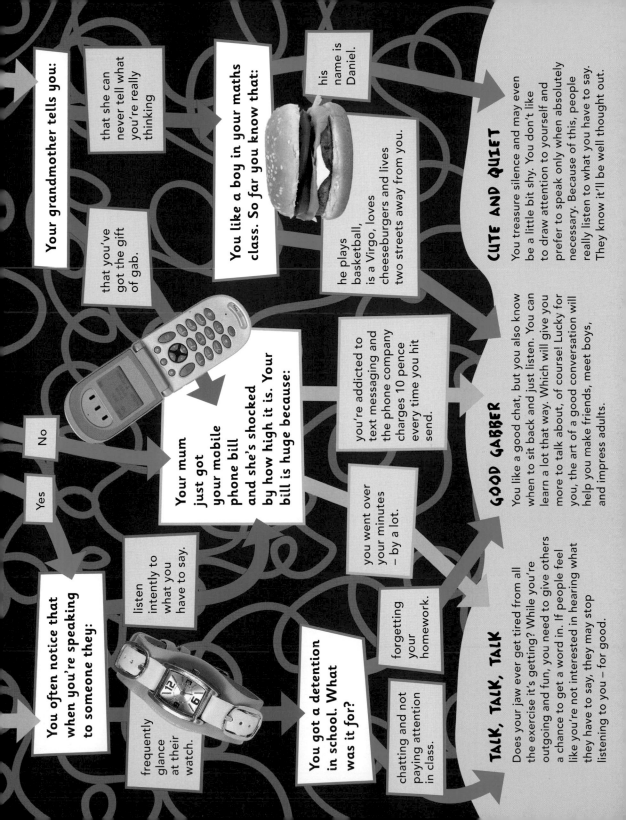

Your grandmother tells you:

that she can never tell what you're really thinking

that you've got the gift of gab.

You like a boy in your maths class. So far you know that:

his name is Daniel.

he plays basketball, is a Virgo, loves cheeseburgers and lives two streets away from you.

Yes

No

Your mum just got your mobile phone bill and she's shocked by how high it is. Your bill is huge because:

you're addicted to text messaging and the phone company charges 10 pence every time you hit send.

you went over your minutes – by a lot.

You often notice that when you're speaking to someone they:

listen intently to what you have to say.

frequently glance at their watch.

You got a detention in school. What was it for?

forgetting your homework.

chatting and not paying attention in class.

CUTE AND QUIET

You treasure silence and may even be a little bit shy. You don't like to draw attention to yourself and prefer to speak only when absolutely necessary. Because of this, people really listen to what you have to say. They know it'll be well thought out.

GOOD GABBER

You like a good chat, but you also know when to sit back and just listen. You can learn a lot that way. Which will give you more to talk about, of course! Lucky for you, the art of a good conversation will help you make friends, meet boys, and impress adults.

TALK, TALK, TALK

Does your jaw ever get tired from all the exercise it's getting? While you're outgoing and fun, you need to give others a chance to get a word in. If people feel like you're not interested in hearing what they have to say, they may stop listening to you – for good.

Confident or Conceited?

It's great to believe in yourself, but are you becoming too cool for school?

1 **You won the debate club contest at school. When the other team congratulates you, you say:**

a. "Thanks, but was there ever any doubt who would win?"

b. "There must be some mistake. I thought my speech was terrible."

c. "Thanks, I worked really hard for this. You did a great job, too."

2 **You come to school in a new skirt that you love. When your friends pay you compliments, you say:**

a. "Isn't it fabulous? I look great in it, don't I?

b. "Are you sure this is the right colour for me?"

c. "I love the way this outfit makes me feel."

3 **You've got a huge science project due tomorrow. You:**

a. are confident that you'll do well. You always do.

b. are dreading it all day. Science is so hard!

c. spend a lot of time on it and make sure everything is finished and perfected.

4 **You have long, thick, shiny hair. When someone compliments you on it, you:**

a. agree that your hair is probably your best feature.

b. are surprised that they think your rat's nest looks good.

c. say thank you and smile appreciatively.

5 **Football trials are tomorrow and all of your friends are panicking about them. You:**

a. offer to help perfect their dribbling skills since you clearly know the secret.

b. are panicking too. Everyone else is so much better than you are.

c. suggest that you all get together for an extra practice session after school.

6 You bought a new bikini without even trying it on because:

a. you know you will look good.

b. dressing rooms are so embarrassing.

c. you know what your size is.

7 You have a really cool set of bracelets and you buy the same ones for your friend. You do this because:

a. she worships you and wants everything you own.

b. you can't think of anything else to get her.

c. she admired them once when you were wearing them.

8 A friend's mum compliments you on what a great dancer you are. You say:

a. "Yeah, I think I will be a professional dancer someday."

b. "Ugh, I have no rhythm whatsoever."

c. "Thanks. I love to dance."

ANSWERS

Mostly A's
A Little Arrogant

Being sure of yourself isn't a bad thing, but being too pleased with yourself can be. It's a turn off being around someone who thinks they can do no wrong. When someone gives you a compliment, simply say thank you and move on. Better yet, say something nice right back!

Mostly B's
So Little Self-Esteem

Do you like anything about yourself? Take a moment to think about your unique or strong qualities. Are you a loyal friend? A really good speller? Can you make other people laugh? All people have talents and attributes that make them special – including you.

Mostly C's
Seriously Self-Assured

You know you're a special person and that knowledge allows you to do many things. But you're not conceited and you don't flaunt your fabulousness, which makes people flock to you. Your friends want to be like you because you always know the right thing to say or do in any situation.

What is in Your Dream House?

Is it filled with priceless antiques or super stylish gear? See what your home décor says about you!

1 You walk in the door of your house. What's the first thing you see?

a. A vase filled with beautiful bamboo shoots

b. A huge closet

c. A great piece of art hanging on the wall

2 Your kitchen is:

a. bright and airy with copper pots and pans hanging from the ceiling.

b. small and chic. You're not really interested in cooking.

c. sleek and modern with a huge cooker and a fridge full of food.

3 The most prominent colors on display are:

a. reds and yellows.

b. black and white.

c. greens and blues.

4 Go into the living room. Your sofa is:

a. large and comfy with lots of cushions strewn about.

b. luxurious and made of leather.

c. a distinct shape, with matching chairs.

5 Is there a TV?

a. Yes, but it's small

b. Yes, a flat screen that hangs on the wall

c. Yes, but it's hidden behind a nice piece of furniture

6 What about books? Where are they?

a. All over the house. You're running out of room!

b. In a large bookcase that takes up one entire wall

c. On your coffee table as part of the décor

9 Go outside. What's in the back garden?

a. A vegetable garden

b. A swimming pool

c. A rock garden and goldfish pond

ANSWERS

Mostly A's

Cosy Cottage

You're a homebody and your house reflects that. It's filled with lots of knick knacks, comfortable furniture and photos of your favourite moments. Guests feel instantly at ease when they visit you.

7 Are there any family photos displayed?

a. Yes, you have beautifully framed photographs in every room

b. One or two black and white images that were professionally shot

c. They're on table and shelves, but not on the walls

Mostly B's

Oh So Chic

Whatever the newest gadget is, you've got it. You like to live well, so all of your things are very expensive but you don't like clutter. Your home is very organised and is a sign of your success.

8 What kind of bed do you sleep in?

a. A big, fluffy one with a warm duvet

b. A king size one with sheets that exactly match the bedspread

c. A canopy bed with beautiful linens draped down the sides

Mostly C's

Zen Palace

Tranquility is your trademark so your home is a calm place where you can centre yourself after a long day. You love to have friends over to relax and often offer to cook them wonderful meals.

Are You A People Pleaser?

Would you do anything to make your friends and family happy?

1 A friend eats tuna sandwiches every day and the smell makes you feel sick. Today, she brings a sandwich for you too. What do you do?

a. Eat it. You don't want to make her feel bad.

b. Tell her you have already eaten, but you'll eat it later.

c. Tell her how thoughtful she is but you really hate tuna.

2 Your parents went away for the weekend and while they were gone your sister didn't lift a finger around the house. The kitchen is a disaster. You:

a. do a major cleaning before they come home, even though the mess wasn't yours. You don't want your mum to be upset.

b. head to a friend's house. You're not going to be around when your mum explodes.

c. offer to help your sister get the house in order.

3 Your friend wants to see a movie that you've already watched five times. When she begs you to go with her, you:

a. see it for a sixth.

b. decline, unless she agrees to see something you'll both enjoy.

c. tell her to see it without you and then you can meet up to discuss. It's a great film!

4 You and a friend are trying to decide where to eat lunch. You really want Mexican food. When she asks you what you're in the mood for, you say:

a. "Definitely tacos."

b. "Tacos'd be great, but I'm up for anything."

c. "Whatever you choose is fine with me."

5 You're out shopping and you only have time to go to one more shop. You want to look at shoes but your friend wants to hit the sports shop. You:

a. agree to split up and meet in half and hour.

b. beg her to come to with you. You saw some cute boots and you need her opinion.

c. relent and go to the sports shop.

6 You're reading a novel that your aunt recommended. You think it's awful. When she gives you a copy of the author's second book, you:

a. thank her for it and suggest you both talk about it over ice cream when you're done.

b. tell her that you're not loving the first book and don't think you could get through a second.

c. take the book and don't bother to read it. She'll never know.

7 You go to the basketball game to watch your crush play but your best friend is having a crisis and crying in the bathroom. When she calls for you, you:

a. tend to her and keep running into the gym to check the score. He looks so cute in his kit!

b. tell her to snap out of it. Life can't always be about her.

c. spend the entire night consoling her.

8 You hate piano lessons, but you know your parents love to hear you play. When they ask you if you want to continue, you:

a. say of course you would.

b. ask if you can have a few days to think it over.

c. tell them absolutely not.

9 It's Halloween and you and your friends are planning a group costume. You want to go as cats and they want to be punk rockers. You:

a. pick up some purple hair dye. Looks like you're going to need it.

b. suggest a compromise. Cats who rock perhaps?

c. say you already bought your tail and ears, so you're going as a feline.

ANSWERS

1 a=3 b=2 c=1
2 a=3 b=1 c=2
3 a=3 b=1 c=2
4 a=3 b=2 c=1
5 a=2 b=1 c=1
6 a=3 b=3 c=2
7 a=2 b=1 c=3
8 a=3 b=2 c=1
9 a=3 b=2 c=1

22–27 points
Yes, Ma'am!

If you're not okay with something, you shouldn't go along with it just because you don't want to disappoint someone. All you are doing is making yourself miserable. People are a lot more resilient than you think. Try telling them what you really feel. They can take it.

16–21 points
Diplomatic Dame

You want everyone to be content so you're very good at compromising. That's a truly wonderful quality. Just make sure that in the process you also get what you need. Making other people happy is no fun if it leaves you feeling miserable or short-changed.

10–15 points
Don't Give An Inch

You don't care about getting on anyone's good side as long as you get what you want. Standing up for yourself and your beliefs is really important but don't alienate people while doing so. In a healthy relationship, sometimes other people need to come first.

How Self-conscious Are You?

Do you second guess yourself too much?

1 You're singing a solo in your school concert. As you stand on stage, you:

a. feel like you were meant to perform your whole life.

b. wonder if you look as incredibly nervous as you feel.

c. hope you don't have food in your teeth.

2 You go shopping for summer clothes with your mum. She picks out this cute little sundress for you and asks what you think. You:

a. immediately go try it on. You think it might look perfect on you!

b. put it back on the rack. You could never wear something that short.

c. doubt it'll look good, but agree to try it on anyway.

3 You just took your French exam. You're convinced you:

a. passed it.

b. failed it.

c. did okay, but not great.

4 You go to school with a new haircut. All day long, you:

a. can't help tossing your head around. You love your new do! You feel great!

b. wonder if people are talking about how bad it looks.

c. can't wait to see your friends and get their opinions.

5 You're getting ready to go to a party. What do you wear?

a. Jeans and a pretty top

b. After changing your outfit seven times, you decide you have nothing to wear and end up staying home

c. An outfit you got a few years ago. You hope you don't look uncool.

answers

Mostly A's
Solid Self-Esteem

You're not self-conscious at all. You know your strengths and your faults (not that you have many!) and love yourself for being you. You look and feel great and it shows and that's what makes you such a joy to be around.

Mostly B's
Utterly Unsure

You focus so much on what you think is wrong with you that you can't see what's right. Try concentrating on all of the things you do well whenever self-doubt starts creeping in. You'll feel better in a flash.

Mostly C's
Dabbles In Doubt

You're pretty confident, but every now and then your positive attitude gets shaken. Don't worry. It happens to the best of us. Just keep believing in yourself and you'll re-realize how truly great you are.

What's Your Secret **TALENT**?

Everybody's got one. Find out yours.

1 Your best subject in school is:

a. maths.

b. English.

c. history.

2 You excel at:

a. sports.

b. art.

c. games that require a lot of thinking like Scrabble or backgammon.

3 You can have any part in the school play. You choose:

a. stage manager.

b. set designer.

c. playwright.

4 People like you because you:

a. always know what to do in a crisis.

b. are really funny.

c. are super clever.

5 You're in a department store. You head straight for:

a. the electronic devices.

b. the scrapbooks and frames.

c. the books.

6 In your spare time, you like to:

a. explore outside.

b. draw or make jewelry.

c. read or write stories.

7 You think you'd make a good:

a. advertising executive or publicist.

b. sculptor or chef.

c. professor or journalist.

ANSWERS

Mostly A's
LOVES TO LEAD

You are: persuasive. You know exactly how to get people to do what you want them to. You could shoot straight to the top and maybe even become the CEO of a huge company. There are no limits for you.

Mostly B's
COMPLETELY CRAFTY

You are: artistic. You love to use your hands to create things, whether it is a painting, hand-knitted scarf, or collage of pictures. You'd make a great fashion stylist, interior designer or architect someday.

Mostly C's
SMART AND SAVVY

You are: clever. You are extremely intelligent and have brainpower to spare, but not in a way that makes others feel stupid. You would be a great lawyer because you know how to use lots of facts to craft

Photo Credits

DK would like to thank the following for their kind permission to reproduce their photographs:

COVER: Adira Edmund/Dreamstime.com (orange Butterfly), Stephen Oliver © Dorling Kindersley (cello); **2:** istockphoto/David Parsons (boom box); **3:** Angela Coppola © DK Publishing (purse, sunglasses), Stephen Oliver © Dorling Kindersley (daffodil); **4:** Angela Coppola © DK Publishing (earrings, flip flops); **5:** Max Blain/BigStockPhoto.com (nail polish), Lori Martin/BigStockPhoto.com (MP3 player), Stephen Oliver © Dorling Kindersley (Valentine), Angela Coppola © DK Publishing (gloves); **6:** www.oldnavy.com or 1-800-OLD-NAVY for store locations (jeans); **20-21:** Paul-Andre Belle Isle/BigStockPhoto.com (cell phone), Paul Cowan/Dreamstime.com (microscope); **22:** Angela Coppola © DK Publishing (flip flops); **24:** Alex Melnick/BigStockPhoto.com (TV); **25:** Stephen Oliver © Dorling Kindersley (lion); **26:** Stephen Oliver © Dorling Kindersley (ice cream cone); **31:** Stephen Oliver © Dorling Kindersley (long sock); **32:** Liz Van Steenburgh/BigStockPhoto.com (granola bars), istockphoto/Tobias Lauchenauer (sandals); **36:** istockphoto/Kathy McCallum (cookies); **37:** Albert Lozano/BigStockPhoto.com (lock); **46:** Angela Coppola © DK Publishing (hair clips); **49:** Andres Rodriguez/BigStockPhoto.com (piggy bank); **51:** Rosmizan Abu Seman/BigStockPhoto.com (laptop); **52-53:** istockphoto/Melissa Carroll (grill), istockphoto/Cristian Lupu (car); **57:** Stephen Oliver © Dorling Kindersley (first aid kit); **59:** istockphoto/Marc Dietrich (pen holder); **61:** Angela Coppola © DK Publishing (earrings); **62-63:** Helga Kvam/Dreamstime.com (compact); **64:** Dwight Lyman/Dreamstime.com (phone), istockphoto/David Parsons (boom box); **66:** Stephen Oliver © Dorling Kindersley (daffodil); **69:** David Coleman/Dreamstime.com (hair dryer); Eddie Saab/BigStockPhoto.com (bungee jumper); **71:** istockphoto/Sang Nguyen (pacifier); **72-73:** Larysa Dodz/Dreamstime.com (kiss), Max Blain/BigStockPhoto.com (nail polish), Lori Martin/BigStockPhoto.com (MP3 player); **75:** Angela Coppola © DK Publishing (blue bag), istockphoto/Lori Sparkia (lunch bag), Rosmizan Abu Seman/BigStockPhoto.com (pink bag), Radu Razvan/BigStockPhoto.com (red backpack), Laura Frenkel/Dreamstime.com (violin case); **77:** Angela Coppola © DK Publishing (scarf); **78-79:** Stephen Oliver © Dorling Kindersley (ball); **80:** www.Shutterstock.com (movie theater); **83:** Angela Coppola © DK Publishing (bag); **84:** istockphoto/Nancy Louie (sunscreen); **85:** Stephen Oliver © Dorling Kindersley (Valentine); **86-87:** Edyta Pawlowska/Dreamstime.com (cheeseburger), Angela Coppola © DK Publishing (watch); **89:** istockphoto/Amanda Cook (bikini), Angela Coppola © DK Publishing (bracelets); **90:** Isabel Poulin/BigStockPhoto.com (bamboo shoots); **92:** istockphoto/Cathleen Clapper (taco); **94:** Evgeniy Pavlenko/BigStockPhoto.com (red jacket), Graça Victoria/Dreamstime.com (scissors), Dreamstime.com (comb); **95:** Stephen Oliver © Dorling Kindersley (beads); **BACK COVER:** Stephen Oliver © Dorling Kindersley (beach ball), Angela Coppola © DK Publishing (flip flops, hat), Holger Wulschlaeger/Dreamstime.com (green butterfly).

All other images © Dorling Kindersley
For further information, see www.dkimages.com